Henry Wadsworth Longfellow

Flower - de - luce and Three Books of Song

Henry Wadsworth Longfellow

Flower - de - luce and Three Books of Song

ISBN/EAN: 9783741178818

Manufactured in Europe, USA, Canada, Australia, Japa

Cover: Foto ©Andreas Hilbeck / pixelio.de

Manufactured and distributed by brebook publishing software (www.brebook.com)

Henry Wadsworth Longfellow

Flower - de - luce and Three Books of Song

COLLECTION
OF
BRITISH AUTHORS

TAUCHNITZ EDITION.

VOL. 1360.

FLOWER-DE-LUCE AND THREE BOOKS OF SONG
BY
HENRY WADSWORTH LONGFELLOW.

IN ONE VOLUME.

FLOWER-DE-LUCE

AND

THREE BOOKS OF SONG.

BY

HENRY WADSWORTH LONGFELLOW.

AUTHORIZED EDITION.

LEIPZIG
BERNHARD TAUCHNITZ
1873.

CONTENTS.

FLOWER-DE-LUCE,
AND OTHER POEMS.
1866.

Flower-de-Luce
Palingenesis
The Bridge of Cloud
Hawthorne
Christmas Bells
The Wind over the Chimney
The Bells of Lynn
Killed at the Ford
Giotto's Tower
To-morrow
Divina Comedia
Noël

THREE BOOKS OF SONG.
BOOK FIRST.
TALES OF A WAYSIDE INN.
THE SECOND DAY.

Prelude
The Sicilian's Tale.
    The Bell of Atri
Interlude
The Spanish Jew's Tale.
    Kambalu
Interlude
The Student's Tale
    The Cobbler of Hagenau

	Page
Interlude	85
The Musician's Tale.	
The Ballad of Carmilhan	89
Interlude	103
The Poet's Tale.	
Lady Wentworth	106
Interlude	115
The Theologian's Tale.	
The Legend Beautiful	117
Interlude	124
The Student's Second Tale.	
The Baron of St. Castine	127
Finale	140

BOOK SECOND.

JUDAS MACCABÆUS	145

BOOK THIRD.
A HANDFUL OF TRANSLATIONS.

The Fugitive	203
The Siege of Kazan	209
The Boy and the Brook	211
To the Stork	213
Consolation	215
To Cardinal Richelieu	218
The Angel and the Child	220
To Italy	223
Wanderer's Night-Songs	224
Remorse	226
Santa Teresa's Book-Mark	228

INTERLUDES AND FINALE OF CHRISTUS.

I. The Abbot Joachim	231
II. Martin Luther	240
III. Finale	251

FLOWER-DE-LUCE,

AND OTHER POEMS.

1866.

FLOWER-DE-LUCE.

BEAUTIFUL lily, dwelling by still rivers,
   Or solitary mere,
Or where the sluggish meadow-brook delivers
   Its waters to the weir!

Thou laughest at the mill, the whir and worry
   Of spindle and of loom,
And the great wheel that toils amid the hurry
   And rushing of the flume.

Born to the purple, born to joy and pleasure,
   Thou dost not toil nor spin,
But makest glad and radiant with thy presence
   The meadow and the lin.

The wind blows, and uplifts thy drooping banner,
   And round thee throng and run

The rushes, the green yeomen of thy manor,
    The outlaws of the sun.

The burnished dragon-fly is thine attendant,
    And tilts against the field,
And down the listed sunbeam rides resplendent
    With steel-blue mail and shield.

Thou art the Iris, fair among the fairest,
    Who, armed with golden rod
And winged with the celestial azure, bearest
    The message of some God.

Thou art the Muse, who far from crowded cities
    Hauntest the sylvan streams,
Playing on pipes of reed the artless ditties
    That come to us as dreams.

O flower-de-luce, bloom on, and let the river
    Linger to kiss thy feet!
O flower of song, bloom on, and make forever
    The world more fair and sweet.

PALINGENESIS.

I LAY upon the headland-height, and listened
To the incessant sobbing of the sea
    In caverns under me,
And watched the waves, that tossed and fled and
    glistened,
Until the rolling meadows of amethyst
    Melted away in mist.

Then suddenly, as one from sleep, I started;
For round about me all the sunny capes
    Seemed peopled with the shapes
Of those whom I had known in days departed,
Apparelled in the loveliness which gleams
    On faces seen in dreams.

A moment only, and the light and glory
Faded away, and the disconsolate shore
    Stood lonely as before;
And the wild-roses of the promontory
Around me shuddered in the wind, and shed
    Their petals of pale red.

There was an old belief that in the embers
Of all things their primordial form exists,
    And cunning alchemists
Could re-create the rose with all its members
From its own ashes, but without the bloom,
    Without the lost perfume.

Ah me! what wonder-working, occult science
Can from the ashes in our hearts once more
    The rose of youth restore?
What craft of alchemy can bid defiance
To time and change, and for a single hour
    Renew this phantom-flower?

"O, give me back," I cried, "the vanished splendors,
The breath of morn, and the exultant strife,
    When the swift stream of life
Bounds o'er its rocky channel, and surrenders
The pond, with all its lilies, for the leap
    Into the unknown deep!"

And the sea answered, with a lamentation,
Like some old prophet wailing, and it said,
    "Alas! thy youth is dead!
It breathes no more, its heart has no pulsation;
In the dark places with the dead of old
    It lies forever cold!"

Then said I, "From its consecrated cerements
I will not drag this sacred dust again,
    Only to give me pain;
But, still remembering all the lost endearments,
Go on my way, like one who looks before,
    And turns to weep no more."

Into what land of harvests, what plantations
Bright with autumnal foliage and the glow
    Of sunsets burning low;
Beneath what midnight skies, whose constellations
Light up the spacious avenues between
    This world and the unseen!

Amid what friendly greetings and caresses,
What households, though not alien, yet not mine,
    What bowers of rest divine;
To what temptations in lone wildernesses,
What famine of the heart, what pain and loss,
    The bearing of what cross!

I do not know; nor will I vainly question
Those pages of the mystic book which hold
    The story still untold,
But without rash conjecture or suggestion
Turn its last leaves in reverence and good heed,
    Until "The End" I read.

THE BRIDGE OF CLOUD.

Burn, O evening hearth, and waken
    Pleasant visions, as of old!
Though the house by winds be shaken,
    Safe I keep this room of gold!

Ah, no longer wizard Fancy
    Builds her castles in the air,
Luring me by necromancy
    Up the never-ending stair!

But, instead, she builds me bridges
    Over many a dark ravine,
Where beneath the gusty ridges
    Cataracts dash and roar unseen.

And I cross them, little heeding
    Blast of wind or torrent's roar,

As I follow the receding
  Footsteps that have gone before.

Naught avails the imploring gesture,
  Naught avails the cry of pain!
When I touch the flying vesture,
  'Tis the gray robe of the rain.

Baffled I return, and, leaning
  O'er the parapets of cloud,
Watch the mist that intervening
  Wraps the valley in its shroud.

And the sounds of life ascending
  Faintly, vaguely, meet the ear,
Murmur of bells and voices blending
  With the rush of waters near.

Well I know what there lies hidden,
  Every tower and town and farm,
And again the land forbidden
  Reassumes its vanished charm.

THE BRIDGE OF CLOUD.

Well I know the secret places,
    And the nests in hedge and tree;
At what doors are friendly faces,
    In what hearts are thoughts of me.

Through the mist and darkness sinking,
    Blown by wind and beaten by shower,
Down I fling the thought I'm thinking,
    Down I toss this Alpine flower.

HAWTHORNE.

MAY 23, 1864.

How beautiful it was, that one bright day
    In the long week of rain!
Though all its splendor could not chase away
    The omnipresent pain.

The lovely town was white with apple-blooms,
    And the great elms o'erhead
Dark shadows wove on their aerial looms,
    Shot through with golden thread.

Across the meadows, by the gray old manse,
    The historic river flowed:
I was as one who wanders in a trance,
    Unconscious of his road.

The faces of familiar friends seemed strange:
    Their voices I could hear,
And yet the words they uttered seemed to change
    Their meaning to my ear.

For the one face I looked for was not there,
    The one low voice was mute;
Only an unseen presence filled the air,
    And baffled my pursuit.

Now I look back, and meadow, manse, and stream
    Dimly my thought defines:
I only see—a dream within a dream—
    The hill-top hearsed with pines.

I only hear above his place of rest
    Their tender undertone,
The infinite longings of a troubled breast,
    The voice so like his own.

There in seclusion and remote from men
    The wizard hand lies cold,

Which at its topmost speed let fall the pen,
  And left the tale half told.

Ah! who shall lift that wand of magic power,
  And the lost clew regain?
The unfinished window in Aladdin's tower
  Unfinished must remain!

CHRISTMAS BELLS.

I HEARD the bells on Christmas Day
Their old, familiar carols play,
    And wild and sweet
    The words repeat
Of peace on earth, good-will to men!

And thought how, as the day had come,
The belfries of all Christendom
    Had rolled along
    The unbroken song
Of peace on earth, good-will to men!

Till, ringing, singing on its way,
The world revolved from night to day,
    A voice, a chime,
    A chant sublime
Of peace on earth, good-will to men!

Then from each black, accursed mouth
The cannon thundered in the South,
    And with the sound
    The carols drowned
Of peace on earth, good-will to men!

It was as if an earthquake rent
The hearth-stones of a continent,
    And made forlorn
    The households born
Of peace on earth, good-will to men!

And in despair I bowed my head;
"There is no peace on earth," I said;
    "For hate is strong,
    And mocks the song
Of peace on earth, good-will to men!"

Then pealed the bells more loud and deep:
"God is not dead; nor doth he sleep!
    The Wrong shall fail,
    The Right prevail,
With peace on earth, good-will to men!"

THE WIND OVER THE CHIMNEY.

SEE, the fire is sinking low,
Dusky red the embers glow,
   While above them still I cower,
While a moment more I linger,
Though the clock, with lifted finger,
   Points beyond the midnight hour.

Sings the blackened log a tune
Learned in some forgotten June
   From a school-boy at his play,
When they both were young together,
Heart of youth and summer weather
   Making all their holiday.

And the night-wind rising, hark!
How above there in the dark,
   In the midnight and the snow,
Ever wilder, fiercer, grander,
Like the trumpets of Iskander,
   All the noisy chimneys blow!

Every quivering tongue of flame
Seems to murmur some great name,
   Seems to say to me, "Aspire!"
But the night-wind answers, "Hollow
Are the visions that you follow,
   Into darkness sinks your fire!"

Then the flicker of the blaze
Gleams on volumes of old days,
   Written by masters of the art,
Loud through whose majestic pages
Rolls the melody of ages,
   Throb the harp-strings of the heart.

And again the tongues of flame
Start exulting and exclaim:
"These are prophets, bards, and seers;
In the horoscope of nations,
Like ascendant constellations,
They control the coming years."

But the night-wind cries: "Despair!
Those who walk with feet of air
Leave no long-enduring marks;
At God's forges incandescent
Mighty hammers beat incessant,
These are but the flying sparks.

"Dust are all the hands that wrought;
Books are sepulchres of thought;
The dead laurels of the dead
Rustle for a moment only,
Like the withered leaves in lonely
Churchyards at some passing tread."

Suddenly the flame sinks down;
Sink the rumors of renown;
　And alone the night-wind drear
Clamors louder, wilder, vaguer,—
"'Tis the brand of Meleager
　Dying on the hearth-stone here!"

And I answer,—"Though it be,
Why should that discomfort me?
　No endeavor is in vain;
Its reward is in the doing,
And the rapture of pursuing
　Is the prize the vanquished gain."

THE BELLS OF LYNN.

HEARD AT NAHANT.

O CURFEW of the setting sun! O Bells of Lynn!
O requiem of the dying day! O Bells of Lynn!

From the dark belfries of yon cloud-cathedral wafted,
Your sounds aerial seem to float, O Bells of Lynn!

Borne on the evening wind across the crimson twilight,
O'er land and sea they rise and fall, O Bells of Lynn!

The fisherman in his boat, far out beyond the headland,
Listens, and leisurely rows ashore, O Bells of Lynn!

Over the shining sands the wandering cattle homeward
Follow each other at your call, O Bells of Lynn!

The distant light-house hears, and with his flaming
    signal
Answers you, passing the watchword on, O Bells of
    Lynn!

And down the darkening coast run the tumultuous
    surges,
And clap their hands, and shout to you, O Bells of
    Lynn!

Till from the shuddering sea, with your wild incanta-
    tions,
Ye summon up the spectral moon, O Bells of Lynn!

And startled at the sight, like the weird woman of
    Endor,
Ye cry aloud, and then are still, O Bells of Lynn!

KILLED AT THE FORD.

He is dead, the beautiful youth,
The heart of honor, the tongue of truth,
He, the life and light of us all,
Whose voice was blithe as a bugle-call,
Whom all eyes followed with one consent,
The cheer of whose laugh, and whose pleasant word,
Hushed all murmurs of discontent.

Only last night, as we rode along
Down the dark of the mountain gap,
To visit the picket-guard at the ford,
Little dreaming of any mishap,
He was humming the words of some old song:
"Two red roses he had on his cap
And another he bore at the point of his sword."

Sudden and swift a whistling ball
Came out of a wood, and the voice was still;
Something I heard in the darkness fall,
And for a moment my blood grew chill;
I spake in a whisper, as he who speaks
In a room where some one is lying dead;
But he made no answer to what I said.

We lifted him up to his saddle again,
And through the mire and the mist and the rain
Carried him back to the silent camp,
And laid him as if asleep on his bed;
And I saw by the light of the surgeon's lamp
Two white roses upon his cheeks,
And one, just over his heart, blood-red!

And I saw in a vision how far and fleet
That fatal bullet went speeding forth,
Till it reached a town in the distant North,
Till it reached a house in a sunny street,
Till it reached a heart that ceased to beat

Without a murmur, without a cry;
And a bell was tolled in that far-off town,
For one who had passed from cross to crown,
And the neighbors wondered that she should die.

GIOTTO'S TOWER.

How many lives, made beautiful and sweet
  By self-devotion and by self-restraint,
  Whose pleasure is to run without complaint
  On unknown errands of the Paraclete,
Wanting the reverence of unshodden feet,
  Fail of the nimbus which the artists paint
  Around the shining forehead of the saint,
  And are in their completeness incomplete!
In the old Tuscan town stands Giotto's tower,
  The lily of Florence blossoming in stone,—
  A vision, a delight, and a desire,—
The builder's perfect and centennial flower,
  That in the night of ages bloomed alone,
  But wanting still the glory of the spire.

TO-MORROW.

'Tis late at night, and in the realm of sleep
   My little lambs are folded like the flocks;
   From room to room I hear the wakeful clocks
   Challenge the passing hour, like guards that keep
Their solitary watch on tower and steep;
   Far off I hear the crowing of the cocks,
   And through the opening door that time unlocks
   Feel the fresh breathing of To-morrow creep.
To-morrow! the mysterious, unknown guest,
   Who cries to me: "Remember Barmecide,
   And tremble to be happy with the rest."
And I make answer: "I am satisfied;
   I dare not ask; I know not what is best;
   God hath already said what shall betide."

DIVINA COMMEDIA.

I.

Oft have I seen at some cathedral door
    A laborer, pausing in the dust and heat,
    Lay down his burden, and with reverent feet
    Enter, and cross himself, and on the floor
Kneel to repeat his paternoster o'er;
    Far off the noises of the world retreat;
    The loud vociferations of the street
    Become an undistinguishable roar.
So, as I enter here from day to day,
    And leave my burden at this minster gate,
    Kneeling in prayer, and not ashamed to pray,
The tumult of the time disconsolate
    To inarticulate murmurs dies away,
    While the eternal ages watch and wait.

II.

How strange the sculptures that adorn these towers!
   This crowd of statues, in whose folded sleeves
   Birds build their nests; while canopied with leaves
   Parvis and portal bloom like trellised bowers,
And the vast minster seems a cross of flowers!
   But fiends and dragons on the gargoyled eaves
   Watch the dead Christ between the living thieves,
   And, underneath, the traitor Judas lowers!
Ah! from what agonies of heart and brain,
   What exultations trampling on despair,
   What tenderness, what tears, what hate of wrong,
What passionate outcry of a soul in pain,
   Uprose this poem of the earth and air
   This mediæval miracle of song

III.

I ENTER, and I see thee in the gloom
   Of the long aisles, O poet saturnine!
   And strive to make my steps keep pace with thine.
   The air is filled with some unknown perfume;
The congregation of the dead make room
   For thee to pass; the votive tapers shine;
   Like rooks that haunt Ravenna's groves of pine
   The hovering echoes fly from tomb to tomb.
From the confessionals I hear arise
   Rehearsals of forgotten tragedies,
   And lamentations from the crypts below;
And then a voice celestial, that begins
   With the pathetic words, "Although your sins
   As scarlet be," and ends with "as the snow."

IV.

With snow-white veil, and garments as of flame,
   She stands before thee, who so long ago
   Filled thy young heart with passion and the woe
   From which thy song in all its splendors came;
And while with stern rebuke she speaks thy name,
   The ice about thy heart melts as the snow
   On mountain heights, and in swift overflow
   Comes gushing from thy lips in sobs of shame.
Thou makest full confession; and a gleam,
   As of the dawn, on some dark forest cast,
   Seems on thy lifted forehead to increase;
Lethe and Eunoe—the remembered dream
   And the forgotten sorrow—bring at last
   That perfect pardon which is perfect peace.

V.

I LIFT mine eyes, and all the windows blaze
    With forms of saints and holy men who died,
    Here martyred and hereafter glorified;
    And the great Rose upon its leaves displays
Christ's Triumph, and the angelic roundelays,
    With splendor upon splendor multiplied;
    And Beatrice again at Dante's side
    No more rebukes, but smiles her words of praise.
And then the organ sounds, and unseen choirs
    Sing the old Latin hymns of peace and love,
    And benedictions of the Holy Ghost;
And the melodious bells among the spires
    O'er all the house-tops and through heaven above
    Proclaim the elevation of the Host!

VI.

O STAR of morning and of liberty!
   O bringer of the light, whose splendor shines
   Above the darkness of the Apennines,
   Forerunner of the day that is to be!
The voices of the city and the sea,
   The voices of the mountains and the pines,
   Repeat thy song, till the familiar lines
   Are footpaths for the thought of Italy!
Thy fame is blown abroad from all the heights,
   Through all the nations, and a sound is heard,
   As of a mighty wind, and men devout,
Strangers of Rome, and the new proselytes,
   In their own language hear thy wondrous word,
   And many are amazed and many doubt.

NOËL.

ENVOYÉ À M. AGASSIZ, LA VEILLE DE NOËL 1864, AVEC UN PANIER DE VINS DIVERS.

> L'Académie en respect,
> Nonobstant l'incorrection,
> A la faveur du sujet,
>   Ture-lure,
> N'y fera point de rature;
> Noël! ture-lure-lure.
>   GUI-BARÔZAI.

QUAND les astres de Noël
Brillaient, palpitaient au ciel,
Six gaillards, et chacun ivre,
Chantaient gaîment dans le givre,
    "Bons amis
Allons donc chez Agassiz!"

Ces illustres Pèlerins
D'Outre-Mer adroits et fins,
Se donnant des airs de prêtre,
A l'envi se vantaient d'être
    "Bons amis
De Jean Rudolphe Agassiz!"

Œil-de-Perdrix, grand farceur,
Sans reproche et sans pudeur,
Dans son patois de Bourgogne,
Bredouillait comme un ivrogne,
    "Bons amis,
J'ai dansé chez Agassiz!"

Verzenay le Champenois,
Bon Français, pointe New-Yorquois,
Mais des environs d'Avize,
Fredonne à mainte reprise,
    "Bons amis,
J'ai chanté chez Agassiz!"

A côté marchait un vieux
Hidalgo, mais non mousseux;
Dans le temps de Charlemagne
Fut son père Grand d'Espagne!
    "Bons amis
J'ai dîné chez Agassiz!"

Derrière eux un Bordelais,
Gascon, s'il en fut jamais,
Parfumé de poésie
Riait, chantait, plein de vie,
    "Bons amis,
J'ai soupé chez Agassiz!"

Avec ce beau cadet roux,
Bras dessus et bras dessous,
Mine altière et couleur terne,
Vint le Sire de Sauterne;
    "Bons amis,
J'ai couché chez Agassiz!"

Mais le dernier de ces preux,
Était un pauvre Chartreux,
Qui disait, d'un ton robuste,
"Bénédictions sur le Juste!
    Bons amis
Bénissons Père Agassiz!"

Ils arrivent trois à trois,
Montent l'escalier de bois
Clopin-clopant! quel gendarme
Peut permettre ce vacarme,
    Bons amis,
A la porte d'Agassiz!

"Ouvrez donc, mon bon Seigneur,
Ouvrez vite et n'ayez peur;
Ouvrez, ouvrez, car nous sommes
Gens de bien et gentilshommes,
    Bons amis
De la famille Agassiz!"

Chut, ganaches! taisez-vous!
C'en est trop de vos glouglous;
Epargnez aux Philosophes
Vos abominables strophes!
    Bons amis,
Respectez mon Agassiz!

THREE BOOKS OF SONG.

BOOK FIRST.
TALES OF A WAYSIDE INN.
THE SECOND DAY.

PRELUDE.

A COLD, uninterrupted rain,
That washed each southern window-pane,
And made a river of the road;
A sea of mist that overflowed
The house, the barns, the gilded vane,
And drowned the upland and the plain,
Through which the oak-trees, broad and high,
Like phantom ships went drifting by;
And, hidden behind a watery screen,
The sun unseen, or only seen
As a faint pallor in the sky;—
Thus cold and colorless and gray,
The morn of that autumnal day,
As if reluctant to begin,
Dawned on the silent Sudbury Inn,
And all the guests that in it lay.

Full late they slept. They did not hear
The challenge of Sir Chanticleer,
Who on the empty threshing-floor,
Disdainful of the rain outside,
Was strutting with a martial stride,
As if upon his thigh he wore
The famous broadsword of the Squire,
And said, "Behold me and admire!"

Only the Poet seemed to hear,
In drowse or dream, more near and near
Across the border-land of sleep
The blowing of a blithesome horn,
That laughed the dismal day to scorn;
A splash of hoofs and rush of wheels
Through sand and mire like stranding keels,
As from the road with sudden sweep
The Mail drove up the little steep,
And stopped beside the tavern door;
A moment stopped, and then again

With crack of whip and bark of dog
Plunged forward through the sea of fog,
And all was silent as before,—
All silent save the dripping rain.

Then one by one the guests came down,
And greeted with a smile the Squire,
Who sat before the parlor fire,
Reading the paper fresh from town.
First the Sicilian, like a bird,
Before his form appeared, was heard
Whistling and singing down the stair;
Then came the Student, with a look
As placid as a meadow-brook;
The Theologian, still perplexed
With thoughts of this world and the next;
The Poet then, as one who seems
Walking in visions and in dreams;
Then the Musician, like a fair
Hyperion from whose golden hair
The radiance of the morning streams;

And last the aromatic Jew
Of Alicant, who, as he threw
The door wide open, on the air
Breathed round about him a perfume
Of damask roses in full bloom,
Making a garden of the room.

The breakfast ended, each pursued
The promptings of his various mood;
Beside the fire in silence smoked
The taciturn, impassive Jew,
Lost in a pleasant reverie;
While, by his gravity provoked,
His portrait the Sicilian drew,
And wrote beneath it "Edrehi,
At the Red Horse in Sudbury."

By far the busiest of them all,
The Theologian in the hall
Was feeding robins in a cage,—
Two corpulent and lazy birds,

Vagrants and pilferers at best,
If one might trust the hostler's words,
Chief instrument of their arrest;
Two poets of the Golden Age,
Heirs of a boundless heritage
Of fields and orchards, east and west,
And sunshine of long summer days,
Though outlawed now and dispossessed!—
Such was the Theologian's phrase.

Meanwhile the Student held discourse
With the Musician, on the source
Of all the legendary lore
Among the nations, scattered wide
Like silt and seaweed by the force
And fluctuation of the tide;
The tale repeated o'er and o'er,
With change of place and change of name,
Disguised, transformed, and yet the same
We've heard a hundred times before.

The Poet at the window mused,
And saw, as in a dream confused,
The countenance of the Sun, discrowned,
And haggard with a pale despair,
And saw the cloud-rack trail and drift
Before it, and the trees uplift
Their leafless branches, and the air
Filled with the arrows of the rain,
And heard amid the mist below,
Like voices of distress and pain,
That haunt the thoughts of men insane,
The fateful cawings of the crow.

Then down the road, with mud besprent,
And drenched with rain from head to hoof,
The rain-drops dripping from his mane
And tail as from a pent-house roof,
A jaded horse, his head down bent,
Passed slowly, limping as he went.

PRELUDE.

The young Sicilian—who had grown
Impatient longer to abide
A prisoner, greatly mortified
To see completely overthrown
His plans for angling in the brook,
And, leaning o'er the bridge of stone,
To watch the speckled trout glide by,
And float through the inverted sky,
Still round and round the baited hook—
Now paced the room with rapid stride,
And, pausing at the Poet's side,
Looked forth, and saw the wretched steed,
And said: "Alas for human greed,
That with cold hand and stony eye
Thus turns an old friend out to die,
Or beg his food from gate to gate!
This brings a tale into my mind,
Which, if you are not disinclined
To listen, I will now relate."

All gave assent; all wished to hear,
Not without many a jest and jeer,
The story of a spavined steed;
And even the Student with the rest
Put in his pleasant little jest
Out of Malherbe, that Pegasus
Is but a horse that with all speed
Bears poets to the hospital;
While the Sicilian, self-possessed,
After a moment's interval
Began his simple story thus.

THE SICILIAN'S TALE.

THE BELL OF ATRI.

At Atri in Abruzzo, a small town
Of ancient Roman date, but scant renown,
One of those little places that have run
Half up the hill, beneath a blazing sun,
And then sat down to rest, as if to say,
"I climb no farther upward, come what may,"—
The Re Giovanni, now unknown to fame,
So many monarchs since have borne the name,
Had a great bell hung in the market-place
Beneath a roof, projecting some small space,
By way of shelter from the sun and rain.
Then rode he through the streets with all his train,
And, with the blast of trumpets loud and long,
Made proclamation, that whenever wrong
Was done to any man, he should but ring
The great bell in the square, and he, the King,

Would cause the Syndic to decide thereon.
Such was the proclamation of King John.

How swift the happy days in Atri sped,
What wrongs were righted, need not here be said.
Suffice it that, as all things must decay,
The hempen rope at length was worn away,
Unravelled at the end, and, strand by strand,
Loosened and wasted in the ringer's hand,
Till one, who noted this in passing by,
Mended the rope with braids of briony,
So that the leaves and tendrils of the vine
Hung like a votive garland at a shrine.

By chance it happened that in Atri dwelt
A knight, with spur on heel and sword in belt,
Who loved to hunt the wild-boar in the woods,
Who loved his falcons with their crimson hoods,
Who loved his hounds and horses, and all sports
And prodigalities of camps and courts;—
Loved, or had loved them; for at last, grown old,
His only passion was the love of gold.

THE BELL OF ATRI.

He sold his horses, sold his hawks and hounds,
Rented his vineyards and his garden-grounds,
Kept but one steed, his favorite steed of all,
To starve and shiver in a naked stall,
And day by day sat brooding in his chair,
Devising plans how best to hoard and spare.

At length he said: "What is the use or need
To keep at my own cost this lazy steed,
Eating his head off in my stables here,
When rents are low and provender is dear?
Let him go feed upon the public ways;
I want him only for the holidays."
So the old steed was turned into the heat
Of the long, lonely, silent, shadeless street;
And wandered in suburban lanes forlorn,
Barked at by dogs, and torn by brier and thorn.

One afternoon, as in that sultry clime
It is the custom in the summer time,
With bolted doors and window-shutters closed,
The inhabitants of Atri slept or dozed;

When suddenly upon their senses fell
The loud alarum of the accusing bell!
The Syndic started from his deep repose,
Turned on his couch, and listened, and then rose
And donned his robes, and with reluctant pace
Went panting forth into the market-place,
Where the great bell upon its cross-beam swung
Reiterating with persistent tongue,
In half-articulate jargon, the old song:
"Some one hath done a wrong, hath done a wrong!"

But ere he reached the belfry's light arcade
He saw, or thought he saw, beneath its shade,
No shape of human form of woman born,
But a poor steed dejected and forlorn,
Who with uplifted head and eager eye
Was tugging at the vines of briony.
"Domeneddio!" cried the Syndic straight,
"This is the Knight of Atri's steed of state!
He calls for justice, being sore distressed,
And pleads his cause as loudly as the best."

Meanwhile from street and lane a noisy crowd
Had rolled together like a summer cloud,
And told the story of the wretched beast
In five-and-twenty different ways at least,
With much gesticulation and appeal
To heathen gods, in their excessive zeal.
The Knight was called and questioned; in reply
Did not confess the fact, did not deny;
Treated the matter as a pleasant jest,
And set at naught the Syndic and the rest,
Maintaining in an angry undertone,
That he should do what pleased him with his own.

And thereupon the Syndic gravely read
The proclamation of the King; then said:
"Pride goeth forth on horseback grand and gay,
But cometh back on foot, and begs its way;
Fame is the fragrance of heroic deeds,
Of flowers of chivalry and not of weeds!
These are familiar proverbs; but I fear
They never yet have reached your knightly ear.

What fair renown, what honor, what repute
Can come to you from starving this poor brute?
He who serves well and speaks not, merits more
Than they who clamor loudest at the door.
Therefore the law decrees that as this steed
Served you in youth, henceforth you shall take heed
To comfort his old age, and to provide
Shelter in stall, and food and field beside."

The Knight withdrew abashed; the people all
Led home the steed in triumph to his stall.
The King heard and approved, and laughed in glee,
And cried aloud: "Right well it pleaseth me!
Church-bells at best but ring us to the door;
But go not in to mass; my bell doth more:
It cometh into court and pleads the cause
Of creatures dumb and unknown to the laws;
And this shall make, in every Christian clime,
The Bell of Atri famous for all time."

INTERLUDE.

"YES, well your story pleads the cause
Of those dumb mouths that have no speech,
Only a cry from each to each
In its own kind, with its own laws;
Something that is beyond the reach
Of human power to learn or teach,—
An inarticulate moan of pain,
Like the immeasurable main
Breaking upon an unknown beach."

Thus spake the Poet with a sigh;
Then added, with impassioned cry,
As one who feels the words he speaks,
The color flushing in his cheeks,
The fervor burning in his eye:

"Among the noblest in the land,
Though he may count himself the least,
That man I honor and revere
Who without favor, without fear,
In the great city dares to stand
The friend of every friendless beast,
And tames with his unflinching hand
The brutes that wear our form and face,
The were-wolves of the human race!"
Then paused, and waited with a frown,
Like some old champion of romance,
Who, having thrown his gauntlet down,
Expectant leans upon his lance;
But neither Knight nor Squire is found
To raise the gauntlet from the ground,
And try with him the battle's chance.

"Wake from your dreams, O Edrehi!
Or dreaming speak to us, and make
A feint of being half awake,

INTERLUDE.

And tell us what your dreams may be.
Out of the hazy atmosphere
Of cloud-land deign to reappear
Among us in this Wayside Inn;
Tell us what visions and what scenes
Illuminate the dark ravines
In which you grope your way. Begin!"

Thus the Sicilian spake. The Jew
Made no reply, but only smiled,
As men unto a wayward child,
Not knowing what to answer, do.
As from a cavern's mouth, o'ergrown
With moss and intertangled vines,
A streamlet leaps into the light
And murmurs over root and stone
In a melodious undertone;
Or as amid the noonday night
Of sombre and wind-haunted pines,
There runs a sound as of the sea;

So from his bearded lips there came
A melody without a name,
A song, a tale, a history,
Or whatsoever it may be,
Writ and recorded in these lines.

THE SPANISH JEW'S TALE.

KAMBALU.

INTO the city of Kambalu,
By the road that leadeth to Ispahan,
At the head of his dusty caravan,
Laden with treasure from realms afar,
Baldacca and Kelat and Kandahar,
Rode the great captain Alaù.

The Khan from his palace-window gazed,
And saw in the thronging street beneath,
In the light of the setting sun, that blazed
Through the clouds of dust by the caravan raised,
The flash of harness and jewelled sheath,
And the shining scymitars of the guard,
And the weary camels that bared their teeth,
As they passed and passed through the gates unbarred
Into the shade of the palace-yard.

Thus into the city of Kambalu
Rode the great captain Alau;
And he stood before the Khan, and said:
"The enemies of my lord are dead;
All the Kalifs of all the West
Bow and obey thy least behest;
The plains are dark with the mulberry-trees,
The weavers are busy in Samarcand,
The miners are sifting the golden sand,
The divers plunging for pearls in the seas,
And peace and plenty are in the land.

"Baldacca's Kalif, and he alone,
Rose in revolt against thy throne:
His treasures are at thy palace-door,
With the swords and the shawls and the jewels he
       wore;
His body is dust o'er the desert blown.

"A mile outside of Baldacca's gate
I left my forces to lie in wait,

Concealed by forests and hillocks of sand,
And forward dashed with a handful of men,
To lure the old tiger from his den
Into the ambush I had planned.
Ere we reached the town the alarm was spread,
For we heard the sound of gongs from within;
And with clash of cymbals and warlike din
The gates swung wide; and we turned and fled;
And the garrison sallied forth and pursued,
With the gray old Kalif at their head,
And above them the banner of Mohammed:
So we snared them all, and the town was subdued.

"As in at the gate we rode, behold,
A tower that is called the Tower of Gold!
For there the Kalif had hidden his wealth,
Heaped and hoarded and piled on high,
Like sacks of wheat in a granary;
And thither the miser crept by stealth
To feel of the gold that gave him health,
And to gaze and gloat with his hungry eye

On jewels that gleamed like a glow-worm's spark,
Or the eyes of a panther in the dark.

"I said to the Kalif: 'Thou art old,
Thou hast no need of so much gold.
Thou shouldst not have heaped and hidden it here,
Till the breath of battle was hot and near,
But have sown through the land these useless hoards
To spring into shining blades of swords,
And keep thine honor sweet and clear.
These grains of gold are not grains of wheat;
These bars of silver thou canst not eat;
These jewels and pearls and precious stones
Cannot cure the aches in thy bones,
Nor keep the feet of Death one hour
From climbing the stairways of thy tower!'

"Then into his dungeon I locked the drone,
And left him to feed there all alone
In the honey-cells of his golden hive:
Never a prayer, nor a cry, nor a groan

KAMBALU.

Was heard from those massive walls of stone,
Nor again was the Kalif seen alive!

"When at last we unlocked the door,
We found him dead upon the floor;
The rings had dropped from his withered hands,
His teeth were like bones in the desert sands:
Still clutching his treasure he had died;
And as he lay there, he appeared
A statue of gold with a silver beard,
His arms outstretched as if crucified."

This is the story, strange and true,
That the great captain Alau
Told to his brother the Tartar Khan,
When he rode that day into Kambalu
By the road that leadeth to Ispahan.

INTERLUDE.

"I THOUGHT before your tale began,"
The Student murmured, "we should have
Some legend written by Judah Rav
In his Gemara of Babylon;
Or something from the Gulistan,—
The tale of the Cazy of Hamadan,
Or of that King of Khorasan
Who saw in dreams the eyes of one
That had a hundred years been dead
Still moving restless in his head,
Undimmed, and gleaming with the lust
Of power, though all the rest was dust.

"But lo! your glittering caravan
On the road that leadeth to Ispahan

Hath led us farther to the East
Into the regions of Cathay.
Spite of your Kalif and his gold,
Pleasant has been the tale you told,
And full of color; that at least
No one will question or gainsay.
And yet on such a dismal day
We need a merrier tale to clear
The dark and heavy atmosphere.
So listen, Lordlings, while I tell,
Without a preface, what befell
A simple cobbler, in the year—
No matter; it was long ago;
And that is all we need to know."

THE STUDENT'S TALE.

THE COBBLER OF HAGENAU.

I TRUST that somewhere and somehow
You all have heard of Hagenau,
A quiet, quaint, and ancient town
Among the green Alsatian hills,
A place of valleys, streams, and mills,
Where Barbarossa's castle, brown
With rust of centuries, still looks down
On the broad, drowsy land below,—
On shadowy forests filled with game,
And the blue river winding slow
Through meadows, where the hedges grow
That give this little town its name.

It happened in the good old times,
While yet the Master-singers filled

THE COBBLER OF HAGENAU.

The noisy workshop and the guild
With various melodies and rhymes,
That here in Hagenau there dwelt
A cobbler,—one who loved debate,
And, arguing from a postulate,
Would say what others only felt;
A man of forecast and of thrift,
And of a shrewd and careful mind
In this world's business, but inclined
Somewhat to let the next world drift.

Hans Sachs with vast delight he read,
And Regenbogen's rhymes of love,
For their poetic fame had spread
Even to the town of Hagenau;
And some Quick Melody of the Plough,
Or Double Harmony of the Dove,
Was always running in his head.
He kept, moreover, at his side,
Among his leathers and his tools,

Reynard the Fox, the Ship of Fools,
Or Eulenspiegel, open wide;
With these he was much edified:
He thought them wiser than the Schools.

His good wife, full of godly fear,
Liked not these worldly themes to hear;
The Psalter was her book of songs;
The only music to her ear
Was that which to the Church belongs,
When the loud choir on Sunday chanted,
And the two angels carved in wood,
That by the windy organ stood,
Blew on their trumpets loud and clear,
And all the echoes, far and near,
Gibbered as if the church were haunted.

Outside his door, one afternoon,
This humble votary of the muse
Sat in the narrow strip of shade

By a projecting cornice made,
Mending the Burgomaster's shoes,
And singing a familiar tune:

  "Our ingress into the world
    Was naked and bare;
  Our progress through the world
    Is trouble and care;
  Our egress from the world
    Will be nobody knows where:
  But if we do well here
    We shall do well there;
  And I could tell you no more,
    Should I preach a whole year!"

Thus sang the cobbler at his work;
And with his gestures marked the time,
Closing together with a jerk
Of his waxed thread the stitch and rhyme.
Meanwhile his quiet little dame

Was leaning o'er the window-sill,
Eager, excited, but mouse-still,
Gazing impatiently to see
What the great throng of folk might be
That onward in procession came,
Along the unfrequented street,
With horns that blew, and drums that beat,
And banners flying, and the flame
Of tapers, and, at times, the sweet
Voices of nuns; and as they sang
Suddenly all the church-bells rang.

In a gay coach, above the crowd,
There sat a monk in ample hood,
Who with his right hand held aloft
A red and ponderous cross of wood,
To which at times he meekly bowed.
In front three horsemen rode, and oft,
With voice and air importunate,
A boisterous herald cried aloud:

"The grace of God is at your gate!"
So onward to the church they passed.

The cobbler slowly turned his last,
And, wagging his sagacious head,
Unto his kneeling housewife said:
"'Tis the monk Tetzel. I have heard
The cawings of that reverend bird.
Don't let him cheat you of your gold;
Indulgence is not bought and sold."

The church of Hagenau, that night,
Was full of people, full of light;
An odor of incense filled the air,
The priest intoned, the organ groaned
Its inarticulate despair;
The candles on the altar blazed,
And full in front of it upraised
The red cross stood against the glare.
Below, upon the altar-rail

Indulgences were set to sale,
Like ballads at a country fair.
A heavy strong-box, iron-bound
And carved with many a quaint device,
Received, with a melodious sound,
The coin that purchased Paradise.

Then from the pulpit overhead,
Tetzel the monk, with fiery glow,
Thundered upon the crowd below.
"Good people all, draw near!" he said;
"Purchase these letters, signed and sealed,
By which all sins, though unrevealed
And unrepented, are forgiven!
Count but the gain, count not the loss!
Your gold and silver are but dross,
And yet they pave the way to heaven.
I hear your mothers and your sires
Cry from their purgatorial fires,
And will ye not their ransom pay?

O senseless people! when the gate
Of heaven is open, will ye wait?
Will ye not enter in to-day?
To-morrow it will be too late;
I shall be gone upon my way.
Make haste! bring money while ye may!"

The women shuddered, and turned pale;
Allured by hope or driven by fear,
With many a sob and many a tear,
All crowded to the altar-rail.
Pieces of silver and of gold
Into the tinkling strong-box fell
Like pebbles dropped into a well;
And soon the ballads were all sold.
The cobbler's wife among the rest
Slipped into the capacious chest
A golden florin; then withdrew,
Hiding the paper in her breast;
And homeward through the darkness went

Comforted, quieted, content;
She did not walk, she rather flew,
A dove that settles to her nest,
When some appalling bird of prey
That scared her has been driven away.

The days went by, the monk was gone,
The summer passed, the winter came;
Though seasons changed, yet still the same
The daily round of life went on;
The daily round of household care,
The narrow life of toil and prayer.
But in her heart the cobbler's dame
Had now a treasure beyond price,
A secret joy without a name,
The certainty of Paradise.
Alas, alas! Dust unto dust!
Before the winter wore away,
Her body in the churchyard lay,
Her patient soul was with the Just!

After her death, among the things
That even the poor preserve with care,—
Some little trinkets and cheap rings,
A locket with her mother's hair,.
Her wedding gown, the faded flowers
She wore upon her wedding day,—
Among these memories of past hours,
That so much of the heart reveal,
Carefully kept and put away,
The Letter of Indulgence lay
Folded, with signature and seal.

Meanwhile the Priest, aggrieved and pained,
Waited and wondered that no word
Of mass or requiem he heard,
As by the Holy Church ordained:
Then to the Magistrate complained,
That as this woman had been dead
A week or more, and no mass said,
It was rank heresy, or at least

Contempt of Church; thus said the Priest;
And straight the cobbler was arraigned.

He came, confiding in his cause,
But rather doubtful of the laws.
The Justice from his elbow-chair
Gave him a look that seemed to say:
"Thou standest before a Magistrate,
Therefore do not prevaricate!"
Then asked him in a business way,
Kindly but cold: "Is thy wife dead?"
The cobbler meekly bowed his head;
"She is" came struggling from his throat
Scarce audibly. The Justice wrote
The words down in a book, and then
Continued, as he raised his pen:
"She is; and hath a mass been said
For the salvation of her soul?
Come, speak the truth! confess the whole!"
The cobbler without pause replied:

"Of mass or prayer there was no need;
For at the moment when she died
Her soul was with the glorified!"
And from his pocket with all speed
He drew the priestly title-deed,
And prayed the Justice he would read.

The Justice read, amused, amazed;
And as he read his mirth increased;
At times his shaggy brows he raised,
Now wondering at the cobbler gazed,
Now archly at the angry Priest.
"From all excesses, sins, and crimes
Thou hast committed in past times
Thee I absolve! And furthermore,
Purified from all earthly taints,
To the communion of the Saints
And to the sacraments restore!
All stains of weakness, and all trace
Of shame and censure I efface;

Remit the pains thou shouldst endure,
And make thee innocent and pure,
So that in dying, unto thee
The gates of heaven shall open be!
Though long thou livest, yet this grace
Until the moment of thy death
Unchangeable continueth!"

Then said he to the Priest: "I find
This document is duly signed
Brother John Tetzel, his own hand.
At all tribunals in the land
In evidence it may be used;
Therefore acquitted is the accused."
Then to the cobbler turned: "My friend,
Pray tell me, didst thou ever read
Reynard the Fox?"—"O yes, indeed!"—
"I thought so. Don't forget the end."

INTERLUDE.

"What was the end? I am ashamed
Not to remember Reynard's fate;
I have not read the book of late;
Was he not hanged?" the Poet said.
The Student gravely shook his head,
And answered: "You exaggerate.
There was a tournament proclaimed,
And Reynard fought with Isegrim
The Wolf, and having vanquished him,
Rose to high honor in the State,
And Keeper of the Seals was named!

At this the gay Sicilian laughed:
"Fight fire with fire, and craft with craft;
Successful cunning seems to be
The moral of your tale," said he.

"Mine had a better, and the Jew's
Had none at all, that I could see;
His aim was only to amuse."

Meanwhile from out its ebon case
His violin the Minstrel drew,
And having turned its strings anew,
Now held it close in his embrace,
And poising in his outstretched hand
The bow, like a magician's wand,
He paused, and said, with beaming face:
"Last night my story was too long;
To-day I give you but a song,
An old tradition of the North;
But first, to put you in the mood,
I will a little while prelude,
And from this instrument draw forth
Something by way of overture."

He played; at first the tones were pure
And tender as a summer night,
The full moon climbing to her height,

INTERLUDE.

The sob and ripple of the seas,
The flapping of an idle sail;
And then by sudden and sharp degrees
The multiplied, wild harmonies
Freshened and burst into a gale;
A tempest howling through the dark,
A crash as of some shipwrecked bark,
A loud and melancholy wail.

Such was the prelude to the tale
Told by the Minstrel; and at times
He paused amid its varying rhymes,
And at each pause again broke in
The music of his violin,
With tones of sweetness or of fear,
Movements of trouble or of calm,
Creating their own atmosphere;
As sitting in a church we hear
Between the verses of the psalm
The organ playing soft and clear,
Or thundering on the startled ear.

THE MUSICIAN'S TALE.

THE BALLAD OF CARMILHAN.

I.

At Stralsund, by the Baltic Sea,
   Within the sandy bar,
At sunset of a summer's day,
Ready for sea, at anchor lay
   The good ship Valdemar.

The sunbeams danced upon the waves,
   And played along her side;
And through the cabin windows streamed
In ripples of golden light, that seemed
   The ripple of the tide.

There sat the captain with his friends,
   Old skippers brown and hale,

Who smoked and grumbled o'er their grog,
And talked of iceberg and of fog,
   Of calm and storm and gale.

And one was spinning a sailor's yarn
   About Klaboterman,
The Kobold of the sea; a sprite
Invisible to mortal sight,
   Who o'er the rigging ran.

Sometimes he hammered in the hold,
   Sometimes upon the mast,
Sometimes abeam, sometimes abaft,
Or at the bows he sang and laughed,
   And made all tight and fast.

He helped the sailors at their work,
   And toiled with jovial din;
He helped them hoist and reef the sails,
He helped them stow the casks and bales,
   And heave the anchor in.

But woe unto the lazy louts,
    The idlers of the crew;
Them to torment was his delight,
And worry them by day and night,
    And pinch them black and blue.

And woe to him whose mortal eyes
    Klaboterman behold.
It is a certain sign of death!—
The cabin-boy here held his breath,
    He felt his blood run cold.

II.

The jolly skipper paused awhile,
    And then again began;
"There is a Spectre Ship," quoth he,
"A Ship of the Dead that sails the sea,
    And is called the Carmilhan.

"A ghostly ship, with a ghostly crew,
  In tempests she appears;
And before the gale, or against the gale,
She sails without a rag of sail,
  Without a helmsman steers.

"She haunts the Atlantic north and south,
  But mostly the mid-sea,
Where three great rocks rise bleak and bare
Like furnace-chimneys in the air,
  And are called the Chimneys Three.

"And ill betide the luckless ship
  That meets the Carmilhan;
Over her decks the seas will leap,
She must go down into the deep,
  And perish mouse and man."

The captain of the Valdemar
  Laughed loud with merry heart.

"I should like to see this ship," said he;
"I should like to find these Chimneys Three,
   That are marked down in the chart.

"I have sailed right over the spot," he said,
   "With a good stiff breeze behind,
When the sea was blue, and the sky was clear,—
You can follow my course by these pinholes here,—
   And never a rock could find."

And then he swore a dreadful oath,
   He swore by the Kingdoms Three,
That, should he meet the Carmilhan,
He would run her down, although he ran
   Right into Eternity!

All this, while passing to and fro,
   The cabin-boy had heard;
He lingered at the door to hear,
And drank in all with greedy ear,
   And pondered every word.

He was a simple country lad,
  But of a roving mind.
"O, it must be like heaven," thought he,
"Those far-off foreign lands to see,
  And fortune seek and find!"

But in the fo'castle, when he heard
  The mariners blaspheme,
He thought of home, he thought of God,
And his mother under the churchyard sod,
  And wished it were a dream.

One friend on board that ship had he;
  'Twas the Klaboterman,
Who saw the Bible in his chest,
And made a sign upon his breast,
  All evil things to ban.

III.

The cabin windows have grown blank
  As eyeballs of the dead;
No more the glancing sunbeams burn
On the gilt letters of the stern,
  But on the figure-head;

On Valdemar Victorious,
  Who looketh with disdain
To see his image in the tide
Dismembered float from side to side,
  And reunite again.

"It is the wind," those skippers said,
  "That swings the vessel so;
It is the wind; it freshens fast,
'Tis time to say farewell at last,
  'Tis time for us to go."

They shook the captain by the hand,
   "Good luck! good luck!" they cried;
Each face was like the setting sun,
As, broad and red, they one by one
   Went o'er the vessel's side.

The sun went down, the full moon rose,
   Serene o'er field and flood;
And all the winding creeks and bays
And broad sea-meadows seemed ablaze,
   The sky was red as blood.

The southwest wind blew fresh and fair,
   As fair as wind could be;
Bound for Odessa, o'er the bar,
With all sail set, the Valdemar
   Went proudly out to sea.

The lovely moon climbs up the sky
   As one who walks in dreams;

A tower of marble in her light,
A wall of black, a wall of white,
  The stately vessel seems.

Low down upon the sandy coast
  The lights begin to burn;
And now, uplifted high in air,
They kindle with a fiercer glare,
  And now drop far astern.

The dawn appears, the land is gone,
  The sea is all around;
Then on each hand low hills of sand
Emerge and form another land;
  She steereth through the Sound.

Through Kattegat and Skager-rack
  She flitteth like a ghost;
By day and night, by night and day,
She bounds, she flies upon her way
  Along the English coast.

Cape Finisterre is drawing near,
  Cape Finisterre is past;
Into the open ocean stream
She floats, the vision of a dream
  Too beautiful to last.

Suns rise and set, and rise, and yet
  There is no land in sight;
The liquid planets overhead
Burn brighter now the moon is dead,
  And longer stays the night.

IV.

And now along the horizon's edge
  Mountains of cloud uprose,
Black as with forests underneath,
Above their sharp and jagged teeth
  Were white as drifted snows.

Unseen behind them sank the sun,
  But flushed each snowy peak
A little while with rosy light
That faded slowly from the sight
  As blushes from the cheek.

Black grew the sky,—all black, all black;
  The clouds were everywhere;
There was a feeling of suspense
In nature, a mysterious sense
  Of terror in the air.

And all on board the Valdemar
  Was still as still could be;
Save when the dismal ship-bell tolled,
As ever and anon she rolled,
  And lurched into the sea.

The captain up and down the deck
  Went striding to and fro;

Now watched the compass at the wheel,
Now lifted up his hand to feel
   Which way the wind might blow.

And now he looked up at the sails,
   And now upon the deep;
In every fibre of his frame
He felt the storm before it came,
   He had no thought of sleep.

Eight bells! and suddenly abaft,
   With a great rush of rain,
Making the ocean white with spume,
In darkness like the day of doom,
   On came the hurricane.

The lightning flashed from cloud to cloud,
   And rent the sky in two;
A jagged flame, a single jet
Of white fire, like a bayonet
   That pierced the eyeballs through.

Then all around was dark again,
  And blacker than before;
But in that single flash of light,
He had beheld a fearful sight,
  And thought of the oath he swore.

For right ahead lay the Ship of the Dead,
  The ghostly Carmilhan!
Her masts were stripped, her yards were bare,
And on her bowsprit, poised in air,
  Sat the Klaboterman.

Her crew of ghosts was all on deck
  Or clambering up the shrouds;
The boatswain's whistle, the captain's hail,
Were like the piping of the gale,
  And thunder in the clouds.

And close behind the Carmilhan
  There rose up from the sea,

As from a foundered ship of stone,
Three bare and splintered masts alone:
   They were the Chimneys Three!

And onward dashed the Valdemar
   And leaped into the dark;
A denser mist, a colder blast,
A little shudder, and she had passed
   Right through the Phantom Bark.

She cleft in twain the shadowy hulk,
   But cleft it unaware;
As when, careering to her nest,
The sea-gull severs with her breast
   The unresisting air.

Again the lightning flashed; again
   They saw the Carmilhan,
Whole as before in hull and spar;
But now on board of the Valdemar
   Stood the Klaboterman.

And they all knew their doom was sealed;
    They knew that death was near;
Some prayed who never prayed before,
And some they wept, and some they swore,
    And some were mute with fear.

Then suddenly there came a shock,
    And louder than wind or sea
A cry burst from the crew on deck,
As she dashed and crashed, a hopeless wreck,
    ' Upon the Chimneys Three.

The storm and night were passed, the light
    To streak the east began;
The cabin-boy, picked up at sea,
Survived the wreck, and only he,
    To tell of the Carmilhan.

INTERLUDE.

When the long murmur of applause
That greeted the Musician's lay
Had slowly buzzed itself away,
And the long talk of Spectre Ships
That followed died upon their lips
And came unto a natural pause,
"These tales you tell are one and all
Of the Old World," the Poet said,
"Flowers gathered from a crumbling wall,
Dead leaves that rustle as they fall;
Let me present you in their stead
Something of our New England earth,
A tale which, though of no great worth,
Has still this merit, that it yields

A certain freshness of the fields,
A sweetness as of home-made bread."

The student answered: "Be discreet;
For if the flour be fresh and sound,
And if the bread be light and sweet,
Who careth in what mill 'twas ground,
Or of what oven felt the heat,
Unless, as old Cervantes said,
You are looking after better bread
Than any that is made of wheat?
You know that people nowadays
To what is old give little praise;
All must be new in prose and verse:
They want hot bread, or something worse,
Fresh every morning, and half baked;
The wholesome bread of yesterday,
Too stale for them, is thrown away,
Nor is their thirst with water slaked."

INTERLUDE.

As oft we see the sky in May
Threaten to rain, and yet not rain,
The Poet's face, before so gay,
Was clouded with a look of pain,
But suddenly brightened up again;
And without further let or stay
He told his tale of yesterday.

THE POET'S TALE.
LADY WENTWORTH.

One hundred years ago, and something more,
In Queen Street, Portsmouth, at her tavern door,
Neat as a pin, and blooming as a rose,
Stood Mistress Stavers in her furbelows,
Just as her cuckoo-clock was striking nine.
Above her head, resplendent on the sign,
The portrait of the Earl of Halifax,
In scarlet coat and periwig of flax,
Surveyed at leisure all her varied charms,
Her cap, her bodice, her white folded arms,
And half resolved, though he was past his prime,
And rather damaged by the lapse of time,
To fall down at her feet, and to declare
The passion that had driven him to despair.

For from his lofty station he had seen
Stavers, her husband, dressed in bottle-green,

Drive his new Flying Stage-coach, four in hand.
Down the long lane, and out into the land,
And knew that he was far upon the way
To Ipswich and to Boston on the Bay!

Just then the meditations of the Earl
Were interrupted by a little girl,
Barefooted, ragged, with neglected hair,
Eyes full of laughter, neck and shoulders bare,
A thin slip of a girl, like a new moon,
Sure to be rounded into beauty soon,
A creature men would worship and adore,
Though now in mean habiliments she bore
A pail of water, dripping, through the street,
And bathing, as she went, her naked feet.

It was a pretty picture, full of grace,—
The slender form, the delicate, thin face;
The swaying motion, as she hurried by;
The shining feet, the laughter in her eye,
That o'er her face in ripples gleamed and glanced,
As in her pail the shifting sunbeam danced:

And with uncommon feelings of delight
The Earl of Halifax beheld the sight.
Not so Dame Stavers, for he heard her say
These words, or thought he did, as plain as day:
"O Martha Hilton! Fie! how dare you go
About the town half dressed, and looking so!"
At which the gypsy laughed, and straight replied:
"No matter how I look; I yet shall ride
In my own chariot, ma'am." And on the child
The Earl of Halifax benignly smiled,
As with her heavy burden she passed on,
Looked back, then turned the corner, and was gone.

What next, upon that memorable day,
Arrested his attention was a gay
And brilliant equipage, that flashed and spun,
The silver harness glittering in the sun,
Outriders with red jackets, lithe and lank,
Pounding the saddles as they rose and sank,
While all alone within the chariot sat
A portly person with three-cornered hat,

A crimson velvet coat, head high in air,
Gold-headed cane, and nicely powdered hair,
And diamond buckles sparkling at his knees,
Dignified, stately, florid, much at ease.
Onward the pageant swept, and as it passed,
Fair Mistress Stavers courtesied low and fast;
For this was Governor Wentworth, driving down
To Little Harbor, just beyond the town,
Where his Great House stood looking out to sea,
A goodly place, where it was good to be.

It was a pleasant mansion, an abode
Near and yet hidden from the great highroad,
Sequestered among trees, a noble pile,
Baronial and colonial in its style;
Gables and dormer-windows everywhere,
And stacks of chimneys rising high in air,—
Pandæan pipes, on which all winds that blew
Made mournful music the whole winter through.
Within, unwonted splendors met the eye,
Panels, and floors of oak, and tapestry;

Carved chimney-pieces, where on brazen dogs
Revelled and roared the Christmas fires of logs;
Doors opening into darkness unawares,
Mysterious passages, and flights of stairs;
And on the walls, in heavy gilded frames,
The ancestral Wentworths with Old-Scripture names.

Such was the mansion where the great man dwelt,
A widower and childless; and he felt
The loneliness, the uncongenial gloom,
That like a presence haunted every room;
For though not given to weakness, he could feel
The pain of wounds, that ache because they heal.

The years came and the years went,—seven in all,
And passed in cloud and sunshine o'er the Hall;
The dawns their splendor through its chambers shed,
The sunsets flushed its western windows red;
The snow was on its roofs, the wind, the rain;
Its woodlands were in leaf and bare again;
Moons waxed and waned, the lilacs bloomed and died,
In the broad river ebbed and flowed the tide,

Ships went to sea, and ships came home from sea,
And the slow years sailed by and ceased to be.

And all these years had Martha Hilton served
In the Great House, not wholly unobserved:
By day, by night, the silver crescent grew,
Though hidden by clouds, her light still shining through;
A maid of all work, whether coarse or fine,
A servant who made service seem divine!
Through her each room was fair to look upon;
The mirrors glistened, and the brasses shone,
The very knocker on the outer door,
If she but passed, was brighter than before.

And now the ceaseless turning of the mill
Of Time, that never for an hour stands still,
Ground out the Governor's sixtieth birthday,
And powdered his brown hair with silver-gray.
The robin, the forerunner of the spring,
The bluebird with his jocund carolling,
The restless swallows building in the eaves,
The golden buttercups, the grass, the leaves,

The lilacs tossing in the winds of May,
All welcomed this majestic holiday!
He gave a splendid banquet, served on plate,
Such as became the Governor of the State,
Who represented England and the King,
And was magnificent in everything.
He had invited all his friends and peers,—
The Pepperels, the Langdons, and the Lears,
The Sparhawks, the Penhallows, and the rest;
For why repeat the name of every guest?
But I must mention one, in bands and gown,
The rector there, the Reverend Arthur Brown
Of the Established Church; with smiling face
He sat beside the Governor and said grace;
And then the feast went on, as others do,
But ended as none other, or but few.

When they had drunk the King, with many a cheer,
The Governor whispered in a servant's ear,
Who disappeared, and presently there stood
Within the room, in perfect womanhood,

LADY WENTWORTH.

A maiden, modest and yet self-possessed,
Youthful and beautiful, and simply dressed.
Can this be Martha Hilton? It must be!
Yes, Martha Hilton, and no other she!
Dowered with the beauty of her twenty years,
How ladylike, how queenlike she appears;
The pale, thin crescent of the days gone by
Is Dian now in all her majesty!
Yet scarce a guest perceived that she was there,
Until the Governor, rising from his chair,
Played slightly with his ruffles, then looked down,
And said unto the Reverend Arthur Brown:
"This is my birthday; it shall likewise be
My wedding-day; and you shall marry me!"

The listening guests were greatly mystified,
None more so than the rector, who replied:
"Marry you? Yes, that were a pleasant task,
Your Excellency; but to whom? I ask."
The Governor answered: "To this lady here;"
And beckoned Martha Hilton to draw near.

She came and stood, all blushes, at his side.
The rector paused. The impatient Governor cried:
"This is the lady; do you hesitate?
Then I command you as Chief Magistrate."
The rector read the service loud and clear:
"Dearly beloved, we are gathered here,"
And so on to the end. At his command
On the fourth finger of her fair left hand
The Governor placed the ring; and that was all:
Martha was Lady Wentworth of the Hall!

INTERLUDE.

WELL pleased the audience heard the tale.
The Theologian said: "Indeed,
To praise you there is little need;
One almost hears the farmer's flail
Thresh out your wheat, nor does there fail
A certain freshness, as you said,
And sweetness as of home-made bread.
But not less sweet and not less fresh
Are many legends that I know,
Writ by the monks of long-ago,
Who loved to mortify the flesh,
So that the soul might purer grow,
And rise to a diviner state;
And one of these—perhaps of all
Most beautiful—I now recall,

And with permission will narrate;
Hoping thereby to make amends
For that grim tragedy of mine,
As strong and black as Spanish wine,
I told last night, and wish almost
It had remained untold, my friends;
For Torquemada's awful ghost
Came to me in the dreams I dreamed,
And in the darkness glared and gleamed
Like a great lighthouse on the coast."

The Student laughing said: "Far more
Like to some dismal fire of bale
Flaring portentous on a hill;
Or torches lighted on a shore
By wreckers in a midnight gale.
No matter; be it as you will,
Only go forward with your tale."

THE THEOLOGIAN'S TALE.

THE LEGEND BEAUTIFUL.

"HADST thou stayed, I must have fled!"
That is what the Vision said.

In his chamber all alone,
Kneeling on the floor of stone,
Prayed the Monk in deep contrition
For his sins of indecision,
Prayed for greater self-denial
In temptation and in trial;
It was noonday by the dial,
And the Monk was all alone.

Suddenly, as if it lightened,
An unwonted splendor brightened
All within him and without him
In that narrow cell of stone;

And he saw the Blessed Vision
Of our Lord, with light Elysian
Like a vesture wrapped about him
Like a garment round him thrown.

Not as crucified and slain,
Not in agonies of pain,
Not with bleeding hands and feet,
Did the Monk his Master see;
But as in the village street,
In the house or harvest-field,
Halt and lame and blind he healed,
When he walked in Galilee.

In an attitude imploring,
Hands upon his bosom crossed,
Wondering, worshipping, adoring,
Knelt the Monk in rapture lost.
Lord, he thought, in heaven that reignest,
Who am I, that thus thou deignest
To reveal thyself to me?
Who am I, that from the centre

Of thy glory thou shouldst enter
This poor cell, my guest to be?

Then amid his exaltation,
Loud the convent bell appalling,
From its belfry calling, calling,
Rang through court and corridor
With persistent iteration
He had never heard before.
It was now the appointed hour
When alike in shine or shower,
Winter's cold or summer's heat,
To the convent portals came
All the blind and halt and lame,
All the beggars of the street,
For their daily dole of food
Dealt them by the brotherhood;
And their almoner was he
Who upon his bended knee,
Rapt in silent ecstasy

Of divinest self-surrender,
Saw the Vision and the Splendor.

Deep distress and hesitation
Mingled with his adoration;
Should he go, or should he stay?
Should he leave the poor to wait
Hungry at the convent gate,
Till the Vision passed away?
Should he slight his radiant guest,
Slight this visitant celestial,
For a crowd of ragged, bestial
Beggars at the convent gate?
Would the Vision there remain?
Would the Vision come again?

Then a voice within his breast
Whispered, audible and clear
As if to the outward ear:
"Do thy duty; that is best;
Leave unto thy Lord the rest!"

Straightway to his feet he started,
And with longing look intent
On the Blessed Vision bent,
Slowly from his cell departed,
Slowly on his errand went.

At the gate the poor were waiting,
Looking through the iron grating,
With that terror in the eye
That is only seen in those
Who amid their wants and woes
Hear the sound of doors that close,
And of feet that pass them by;
Grown familiar with disfavor,
Grown familiar with the savor
Of the bread by which men die!
But to-day, they knew not why,
Like the gate of Paradise
Seemed the convent gate to rise,
Like a sacrament divine
Seemed to them the bread and wine.

In his heart the Monk was praying,
Thinking of the homeless poor,
What they suffer and endure;
What we see not, what we see;
And the inward voice was saying:
"Whatsoever thing thou doest
To the least of mine and lowest,
That thou doest unto me!"

Unto me! but had the Vision
Come to him in beggar's clothing,
Come a mendicant imploring,
Would he then have knelt adoring,
Or have listened with derision,
And have turned away with loathing?

Thus his conscience put the question,
Full of troublesome suggestion,
As at length, with hurried pace,
Towards his cell he turned his face,

And beheld the convent bright
With a supernatural light,
Like a luminous cloud expanding
Over floor and wall and ceiling.

But he paused with awe-struck feeling
At the threshold of his door,
For the Vision still was standing
As he left it there before,
When the convent bell appalling,
From its belfry calling, calling,
Summoned him to feed the poor.
Through the long hour intervening
It had waited his return,
And he felt his bosom burn,
Comprehending all the meaning,
When the Blessed Vision said,
"Hadst thou stayed, I must have fled!"

INTERLUDE.

ALL praised the Legend more or less;
Some liked the moral, some the verse;
Some thought it better, and some worse
Than other legends of the past;
Until, with ill-concealed distress
At all their cavilling, at last
The Theologian gravely said:
"The Spanish proverb, then, is right;
Consult your friends on what you do,
And one will say that it is white,
And others say that it is red."
And "Amen!" quoth the Spanish Jew.

"Six stories told! We must have seven,
A cluster like the Pleiades,

And lo! it happens, as with these,
That one is missing from our heaven.
Where is the Landlord? Bring him here;
Let the Lost Pleiad reappear."

Thus the Sicilian cried, and went
Forthwith to seek his missing star,
But did not find him in the bar,
A place that landlords most frequent,
Nor yet beside the kitchen fire,
Nor up the stairs, nor in the hall;
It was in vain to ask or call,
There were no tidings of the Squire.

So he came back with downcast head,
Exclaiming: "Well, our bashful host
Hath surely given up the ghost.
Another proverb says the dead
Can tell no tales; and that is true.
It follows, then, that one of you

Must tell a story in his stead.
You must," he to the Student said,
"Who know so many of the best,
And tell them better than the rest."

Straight, by these flattering words beguiled,
The Student, happy as a child
When he is called a little man,
Assumed the double task imposed,
And without more ado unclosed
His smiling lips, and thus began.

THE STUDENT'S SECOND TALE.

THE BARON OF ST. CASTINE.

BARON CASTINE of St. Castine
Has left his château in the Pyrenees,
And sailed across the western seas.
When he went away from his fair demesne
The birds were building, the woods were green;
And now the winds of winter blow
Round the turrets of the old château,
The birds are silent and unseen,
The leaves lie dead in the ravine,
And the Pyrenees are white with snow.

His father, lonely, old, and gray,
Sits by the fireside day by day,
Thinking ever one thought of care;

Through the southern windows, narrow and tall,
The sun shines into the ancient hall,
And makes a glory round his hair.
The house-dog, stretched beneath his chair,
Groans in his sleep as if in pain,
Then wakes, and yawns, and sleeps again,
So silent is it everywhere,—
So silent you can hear the mouse
Run and rummage along the beams
Behind the wainscot of the wall;
And the old man rouses from his dreams,
And wanders restless through the house,
As if he heard strange voices call.

His footsteps echo along the floor
Of a distant passage, and pause awhile;
He is standing by an open door
Looking long, with a sad, sweet smile,
Into the room of his absent son.
There is the bed on which he lay,
There are the pictures bright and gay,

Horses and hounds and sun-lit seas;
There are his powder-flask and gun,
And his hunting-knives in shape of a fan;
The chair by the window where he sat,
With the clouded tiger-skin for a mat,
Looking out on the Pyrenees,
Looking out on Mount Marboré
And the Seven Valleys of Lavedan.
Ah me! he turns away and sighs;
There is a mist before his eyes.

At night, whatever the weather be,
Wind or rain or starry heaven,
Just as the clock is striking seven,
Those who look from the windows see
The village Curate, with lantern and maid,
Come through the gateway from the park
And cross the court-yard damp and dark,—
A ring of light in a ring of shade.
And now at the old man's side he stands,
His voice is cheery, his heart expands,

He gossips pleasantly, by the blaze
Of the fire of fagots, about old days,
And Cardinal Mazarin and the Fronde,
And the Cardinal's nieces fair and fond,
And what they did, and what they said,
When they heard his Eminence was dead.

And after a pause the old man says,
His mind still coming back again
To the one sad thought that haunts his brain,
"Are there any tidings from over sea?
Ah, why has that wild boy gone from me?"
And the Curate answers, looking down,
Harmless and docile as a lamb,
"Young blood! young blood! It must so be!"
And draws from the pocket of his gown
A handkerchief like an oriflamb,
And wipes his spectacles, and they play
Their little game of lansquenet
In silence for an hour or so,
Till the clock at nine strikes loud and clear

From the village lying asleep below,
And across the court-yard, into the dark
Of the winding pathway in the park,
Curate and lantern disappear,
And darkness reigns in the old château.

The ship has come back from over sea,
She has been signalled from below,
And into the harbor of Bordeaux
She sails with her gallant company.
But among them is nowhere seen
The brave young Baron of St. Castine;
He hath tarried behind, I ween,
In the beautiful land of Acadie!

And the father paces to and fro
Through the chambers of the old château,
Waiting, waiting to hear the hum
Of wheels on the road that runs below,
Of servants hurrying here and there,
The voice in the court-yard, the step on the stair,
Waiting for some one who doth not come!

But letters there are, which the old man reads
To the Curate, when he comes at night,
Word by word, as an acolyte
Repeats his prayers and tells his beads;
Letters full of the rolling sea,
Full of a young man's joy to be
Abroad in the world, alone and free;
Full of adventures and wonderful scenes
Of hunting the deer through forests vast
In the royal grant of Pierre du Gast;
Of nights in the tents of the Tarratines;
Of Madocawando the Indian chief,
And his daughters, glorious as queens,
And beautiful beyond belief;
And so soft the tones of their native tongue,
The words are not spoken, they are sung!

And the Curate listens, and smiling says:
"Ah yes, dear friend! in our young days
We should have liked to hunt the deer
All day amid those forest scenes,

And to sleep in the tents of the Tarratines;
But now it is better sitting here
Within four walls, and without the fear
Of losing our hearts to Indian queens;
For man is fire and woman is tow,
And the Somebody comes and begins to blow."
Then a gleam of distrust and vague surmise
Shines in the father's gentle eyes,
As firelight on a window-pane
Glimmers and vanishes again;
But naught he answers; he only sighs,
And for a moment bows his head;
Then, as their custom is, they play
Their little game of lansquenet,
And another day is with the dead.

Another day, and many a day
And many a week and month depart,
When a fatal letter wings its way
Across the sea, like a bird of prey,
And strikes and tears the old man's heart.

Lo! the young Baron of St. Castine,
Swift as the wind is, and as wild,
Has married a dusky Tarratine,
Has married Madocawando's child!

The letter drops from the father's hand;
Though the sinews of his heart are wrung,
He utters no cry, he breathes no prayer,
No malediction falls from his tongue;
But his stately figure, erect and grand,
Bends and sinks like a column of sand
In the whirlwind of his great despair.
Dying, yes, dying! His latest breath
Of parley at the door of death
Is a blessing on his wayward son.
Lower and lower on his breast
Sinks his gray head; he is at rest;
No longer he waits for any one.

For many a year the old château
Lies tenantless and desolate;

Rank grasses in the court-yard grow,
About its gables caws the crow;
Only the porter at the gate
Is left to guard it, and to wait
The coming of the rightful heir;
No other life or sound is there;
No more the Curate comes at night,
No more is seen the unsteady light,
Threading the alleys of the park;
The windows of the hall are dark,
The chambers dreary, cold, and bare!
At length, at last, when the winter is past,
And birds are building, and woods are green,
With flying skirts is the Curate seen
Speeding along the woodland way,
Humming gayly, "No day is so long
But it comes at last to vesper-song."
He stops at the porter's lodge to say
That at last the Baron of St. Castine
Is coming home with his Indian queen,
Is coming without a week's delay;

And all the house must be swept and clean,
And all things set in good array!
And the solemn porter shakes his head;
And the answer he makes is: "Lackaday
We will see, as the blind man said!"

Alert since first the day began,
The cock upon the village church
Looks northward from his airy perch,
As if beyond the ken of man
To see the ships come sailing on,
And pass the Isle of Oléron,
And pass the Tower of Cordouan.

In the church below is cold in clay
The heart that would have leaped for joy—
O tender heart of truth and trust!—
To see the coming of that day;
In the church below the lips are dust,
Dust are the hands, and dust the feet,
That would have been so swift to meet
The coming of that wayward boy.

At night the front of the old château
Is a blaze of light above and below;
There's a sound of wheels and hoofs in the street,
A cracking of whips, and scamper of feet,
Bells are ringing, and horns are blown,
And the Baron hath come again to his own.
The Curate is waiting in the hall,
Most eager and alive of all
To welcome the Baron and Baroness;
But his mind is full of vague distress,
For he hath read in Jesuit books
Of those children of the wilderness,
And now, good, simple man! he looks
To see a painted savage stride
Into the room, with shoulders bare,
And eagle feathers in her hair,
And around her a robe of panther's hide.

Instead, he beholds with secret shame
A form of beauty undefined,

A loveliness without a name,
Not of degree, but more of kind;
Nor bold nor shy, nor short nor tall,
But a new mingling of them all.
Yes, beautiful beyond belief,
Transfigured and transfused, he sees
The lady of the Pyrenees,
The daughter of the Indian chief.
Beneath the shadow of her hair
The gold-bronze color of the skin
Seems lighted by a fire within,
As when a burst of sunlight shines
Beneath a sombre grove of pines,—
A dusky splendor in the air.
The two small hands, that now are pressed
In his, seem made to be caressed,
They lie so warm and soft and still,
Like birds half hidden in a nest,
Trustful, and innocent of ill.
And ah! he cannot believe his ears
When her melodious voice he hears

Speaking his native Gascon tongue;
The words she utters seem to be
Part of some poem of Goudouli,
They are not spoken, they are sung!
And the Baron smiles, and says, "You see,
I told you but the simple truth;
Ah, you may trust the eyes of youth!"

Down in the village day by day
The people gossip in their way,
And stare to see the Baroness pass
On Sunday morning to early Mass;
And when she kneeleth down to pray,
They wonder, and whisper together, and say,
"Surely this is no heathen lass!"
And in course of time they learn to bless
The Baron and the Baroness.

And in course of time the Curate learns
A secret so dreadful, that by turns
He is ice and fire, he freezes and burns.
The Baron at confession hath said,

That though this woman be his wife,
He hath wed her as the Indians wed,
He hath bought her for a gun and a knife!
And the Curate replies: "O profligate,
O Prodigal Son! return once more
To the open arms and the open door
Of the Church, or ever it be too late.
Thank God, thy father did not live
To see what he could not forgive;
On thee, so reckless and perverse,
He left his blessing, not his curse.
But the nearer the dawn the darker the night,
And by going wrong all things come right;
Things have been mended that were worse,
And the worse, the nearer they are to mend.
For the sake of the living and the dead,
Thou shalt be wed as Christians wed,
And all things come to a happy end."

O sun, that followest the night,
In yon blue sky, serene and pure,

And pourest thine impartial light
Alike on mountain and on moor,
Pause for a moment in thy course,
And bless the bridegroom and the bride!
O Gave, that from thy hidden source
In yon mysterious mountain-side
Pursuest thy wandering way alone,
And leaping down its steps of stone,
Along the meadow-lands demure
Stealest away to the Adour,
Pause for a moment in thy course
To bless the bridegroom and the bride!

The choir is singing the matin song,
The doors of the church are opened wide,
The people crowd, and press, and throng
To see the bridegroom and the bride.
They enter and pass along the nave;
They stand upon the father's grave;
The bells are ringing soft and slow;
The living above and the dead below

Give their blessing on one and twain;
The warm wind blows from the hills of Spain,
The birds are building, the leaves are green,
And Baron Castine of St. Castine
Hath come at last to his own again.

FINALE.

"*Nunc plaudite!*" the Student cried,
When he had finished; "now applaud,
As Roman actors used to say
At the conclusion of a play;"
And rose, and spread his hands abroad,
And smiling bowed from side to side,
As one who bears the palm away.

And generous was the applause and loud,
But less for him than for the sun,
That even as the tale was done
Burst from its canopy of cloud,

And lit the landscape with the blaze
Of afternoon on autumn days,
And filled the room with light, and made
The fire of logs a painted shade.

A sudden wind from out the west
Blew all its trumpets loud and shrill;
The windows rattled with the blast,
The oak-trees shouted as it passed,
And straight, as if by fear possessed,
The cloud encampment on the hill
Broke up, and fluttering flag and tent
Vanished into the firmament,
And down the valley fled amain
The rear of the retreating rain.

Only far up in the blue sky
A mass of clouds, like drifted snow
Suffused with a faint Alpine glow,
Was heaped together, vast and high,
On which a shattered rainbow hung,

Not rising like the ruined arch
Of some aerial aqueduct,
But like a roseate garland plucked
From an Olympian god, and flung
Aside in his triumphal march.

Like prisoners from their dungeon gloom,
Like birds escaping from a snare,
Like school-boys at the hour of play,
All left at once the pent-up room,
And rushed into the open air;
And no more tales were told that day.

BOOK SECOND.
JUDAS MACCABÆUS.

JUDAS MACCABÆUS.

ACT I.

The Citadel of Antiochus at Jerusalem.

SCENE I. ANTIOCHUS; JASON.

ANTIOCHUS.

O ANTIOCH, my Antioch, my city!
Queen of the East! my solace, my delight!
The dowry of my sister Cleopatra
When she was wed to Ptolemy, and now
Won back and made more wonderful by me!
I love thee, and I long to be once more
Among the players and the dancing women
Within thy gates, and bathe in the Orontes,
Thy river and mine. O Jason, my High-Priest,
For I have made thee so, and thou art mine,
Hast thou seen Antioch the Beautiful?

JASON.

Never, my Lord.

ANTIOCHUS.

Then hast thou never seen
The wonder of the world. This city of David
Compared with Antioch is but a village,
And its inhabitants compared with Greeks
Are mannerless boors.

JASON.

They are barbarians,
And mannerless.

ANTIOCHUS.

They must be civilized.
They must be made to have more gods than one;
And goddesses besides.

JASON.

They shall have more.

ANTIOCHUS.

They must have hippodromes, and games, and baths,
Stage-plays and festivals, and most of all
The Dionysia.

JASON.

They shall have them all.

ANTIOCHUS.

By Heracles! but I should like to see
These Hebrews crowned with ivy, and arrayed
In skins of fawns, with drums and flutes and thyrsi,
Revel and riot through the solemn streets
Of their old town. Ha, ha! It makes me merry
Only to think of it!—Thou dost not laugh.

JASON.

Yea, I laugh inwardly.

ANTIOCHUS.

The new Greek leaven
Works slowly in this Israelitish dough!
Have I not sacked the Temple, and on the altar
Set up the statue of Olympian Jove
To Hellenize it?

JASON.

Thou hast done all this.

ANTIOCHUS.

As thou wast Joshua once and now art Jason,
And from a Hebrew hast become a Greek,

So shall this Hebrew nation be translated,
Their very natures and their names be changed,
And all be Hellenized.

    JASON.
      It shall be done.

    ANTIOCHUS.
Their manners and their laws and way of living
Shall all be Greek. They shall unlearn their language,
And learn the lovely speech of Antioch.
Where hast thou been to-day? Thou comest late.

    JASON.
Playing at discus with the other priests
In the Gymnasium.

    ANTIOCHUS.
      Thou hast done well.
There's nothing better for you lazy priests
Than discus-playing with the common people.
Now tell me, Jason, what these Hebrews call me
When they converse together at their games.

    JASON.
Antiochus Epiphanes, my Lord;
Antiochus the Illustrious.

ANTIOCHUS.

O, not that;
That is the public cry; I mean the name
They give me when they talk among themselves,
And think that no one listens; what is that?

JASON.

Antiochus Epimanes, my Lord!

ANTIOCHUS.

Antiochus the Mad! Ay, that is it.
And who hath said it? Who hath set in motion
That sorry jest?

JASON.

The Seven Sons insane
Of a weird woman, like themselves insane.

ANTIOCHUS.

I like their courage, but it shall not save them.
They shall be made to eat the flesh of swine,
Or they shall die. Where are they?

JASON.

In the dungeons
Beneath this tower.

ANTIOCHUS.

             There let them stay and starve,
Till I am ready to make Greeks of them,
After my fashion.

JASON.

             They shall stay and starve.—
My Lord, the Ambassadors of Samaria
Await thy pleasure.

ANTIOCHUS.

             Why not my displeasure?
Ambassadors are tedious. They are men
Who work for their own ends, and not for mine;
There is no furtherance in them. Let them go
To Apollonius, my governor
There in Samaria, and not trouble me.
What do they want?

JASON.

             Only the royal sanction
To give a name unto a nameless temple
Upon Mount Gerizim.

ANTIOCHUS.

    Then bid them enter.
This pleases me, and furthers my designs.
The occasion is auspicious. Bid them enter.

SCENE II. ANTIOCHUS; JASON; *the* SAMARITAN AMBASSADORS.

ANTIOCHUS.

Approach. Come forward; stand not at the door
Wagging your long beards, but demean yourselves
As doth become Ambassadors. What seek ye?

AN AMBASSADOR.

An audience from the King.

ANTIOCHUS.

      Speak, and be brief.
Waste not the time in useless rhetoric.
Words are not things.

AMBASSADOR, *reading*.

   "To King Antiochus,
The God, Epiphanes; a Memorial
From the Sidonians, who live at Sichem."

ANTIOCHUS.

Sidonians?

AMBASSADOR.

Ay, my Lord.

ANTIOCHUS.

Go on, go on!
And do not tire thyself and me with bowing!

AMBASSADOR, *reading*.

"We are a colony of Medes and Persians."

ANTIOCHUS.

No, ye are Jews from one of the Ten Tribes;
Whether Sidonians or Samaritans
Or Jews of Jewry, matters not to me;
Ye are all Israelites, ye are all Jews.
When the Jews prosper, ye claim kindred with them;
When the Jews suffer, ye are Medes and Persians:
I know that in the days of Alexander
Ye claimed exemption from the annual tribute
In the Sabbatic Year, because, ye said,
Your fields had not been planted in that year.

AMBASSADOR, *reading.*

"Our fathers, upon certain frequent plagues,
And following an ancient superstition,
Were long accustomed to observe that day
Which by the Israelites is called the Sabbath,
And in a temple on Mount Gerizim
Without a name, they offered sacrifice.
Now we, who are Sidonians, beseech thee,
Who art our benefactor and our savior,
Not to confound us with these wicked Jews,
But to give royal order and injunction
To Apollonius in Samaria,
Thy governor, and likewise to Nicanor,
Thy procurator, no more to molest us;
And let our nameless temple now be named
The Temple of Jupiter Hellenius."

ANTIOCHUS.

This shall be done. Full well it pleaseth me
Ye are not Jews, or are no longer Jews,
But Greeks; if not by birth, yet Greeks by custom.

Your nameless temple shall receive the name
Of Jupiter Hellenius. Ye may go!

SCENE III. ANTIOCHUS; JASON.

ANTIOCHUS.

My task is easier than I dreamed. These people
Meet me half-way. Jason, didst thou take note
How these Samaritans of Sichem said
They were not Jews? that they were Medes and Persians,
They were Sidonians, anything but Jews?
'Tis of good augury. The rest will follow
Till the whole land is Hellenized.

JASON.

My Lord,
These are Samaritans. The tribe of Judah
Is of a different temper, and the task
Will be more difficult.

ANTIOCHUS.

Dost thou gainsay me?

JASON.

I know the stubborn nature of the Jew.
Yesterday, Eleazer, an old man,
Being fourscore years and ten, chose rather death
By torture than to eat the flesh of swine.

ANTIOCHUS.

The life is in the blood, and the whole nation
Shall bleed to death, or it shall change its faith!

JASON.

Hundreds have fled already to the mountains
Of Ephraim, where Judas Maccabæus
Hath raised the standard of revolt against thee.

ANTIOCHUS.

I will burn down their city, and will make it
Waste as a wilderness. Its thoroughfares
Shall be but furrows in a field of ashes.
It shall be sown with salt as Sodom is!
This hundred and fifty-third Olympiad
Shall have a broad and blood-red seal upon it,
Stamped with the awful letters of my name,

Antiochus the God, Epiphanes!—
Where are those Seven Sons?

     JASON.
        My Lord, they wait
Thy royal pleasure.

     ANTIOCHUS.
        They shall wait no longer!

ACT II.

The Dungeons in the Citadel.

SCENE I. THE MOTHER *of the* SEVEN SONS *alone, listening.*

    THE MOTHER.

BE strong, my heart! Break not till they are dead,
All, all my Seven Sons; then burst asunder,
And let this tortured and tormented soul
Leap and rush out like water through the shards
Of earthen vessels broken at a well.
O my dear children, mine in life and death,

I know not how ye came into my womb;
I neither gave you breath, nor gave you life,
And neither was it I that formed the members
Of every one of you. But the Creator,
Who made the world, and made the heavens above us,
Who formed the generation of mankind,
And found out the beginning of all things,
He gave you breath and life, and will again
Of his own mercy, as ye now regard
Not your own selves, but his eternal law.
I do not murmur, nay, I thank thee, God,
That I and mine have not been deemed unworthy
To suffer for thy sake, and for thy law,
And for the many sins of Israel.
Hark! I can hear within the sound of scourges!
I feel them more than ye do, O my sons!
But cannot come to you. I, who was wont
To wake at night at the least cry ye made,
To whom ye ran at every slightest hurt,—
I cannot take you now into my lap
And soothe your pain, but God will take you all

Into his pitying arms, and comfort you,
And give you rest.

    A VOICE, *within*.

      What wouldst thou ask of us?
Ready are we to die, but we will never
Transgress the law and customs of our fathers.

    THE MOTHER.

It is the voice of my first-born! O brave
And noble boy! Thou hast the privilege
Of dying first, as thou wast born the first.

    THE SAME VOICE, *within*.

God looketh on us, and hath comfort in us;
As Moses in his song of old declared,
He in his servants shall be comforted.

    THE MOTHER.

I knew thou wouldst not fail!—He speaks no more,
He is beyond all pain!

    ANTIOCHUS, *within*.

       If thou eat not
Thou shalt be tortured throughout all the members
Of thy whole body. Wilt thou eat then?

SECOND VOICE, *within.*

          No.

THE MOTHER.

It is Adaiah's voice. I tremble for him.
I know his nature, devious as the wind,
And swift to change, gentle and yielding always
Be steadfast, O my son!

THE SAME VOICE, *within.*

      Thou, like a fury,
Takest us from this present life, but God,
Who rules the world, shall raise us up again
Into life everlasting.

THE MOTHER.

      God, I thank thee
That thou hast breathed into that timid heart
Courage to die for thee. O my Adaiah,
Witness of God! if thou for whom I feared
Canst thus encounter death, I need not fear;
The others will not shrink.

THIRD VOICE, *within.*

      Behold these hands
Held out to thee, O King Antiochus,

Not to implore thy mercy, but to show
That I despise them. He who gave them to me
Will give them back again.

THE MOTHER.

                          O Avilan,
It is thy voice. For the last time I hear it;
For the last time on earth, but not the last.
To death it bids defiance and to torture.
It sounds to me as from another world,
And makes the petty miseries of this
Seem unto me as naught, and less than naught.
Farewell, my Avilan; nay, I should say
Welcome, my Avilan; for I am dead
Before thee. I am waiting for the others.
Why do they linger?

FOURTH VOICE, *within*.

                         It is good, O King,
Being put to death by men, to look for hope
From God, to be raised up again by him.
But thou—no resurrection shalt thou have
To life hereafter.

THE MOTHER.

    Four! already four!
Three are still living; nay, they all are living,
Half here, half there. Make haste, Antiochus,
To reunite us; for the sword that cleaves
These miserable bodies makes a door
Through which our souls, impatient of release,
Rush to each other's arms.

FIFTH VOICE, *within*.

     Thou hast the power;
Thou doest what thou wilt. Abide awhile,
And thou shalt see the power of God, and how
He will torment thee and thy seed.

THE MOTHER.

      O hasten;
Why dost thou pause? Thou who hast slain already
So many Hebrew women, and hast hung
Their murdered infants round their necks, slay me,
For I too am a woman, and these boys
Are mine. Make haste to slay us all,
And hang my lifeless babes about my neck.

SIXTH VOICE, *within.*

Think not, Antiochus, that takest in hand
To strive against the God of Israel,
Thou shalt escape unpunished, for his wrath
Shall overtake thee and thy bloody house.

THE MOTHER.

One more, my Sirion, and then all is ended.
Having put all to bed, then in my turn
I will lie down and sleep as sound as they.
My Sirion, my youngest, best beloved!
And those bright golden locks, that I so oft
Have curled about these fingers, even now
Are foul with blood and dust, like a lamb's fleece,
Slain in the shambles.—Not a sound I hear.
This silence is more terrible to me
Than any sound, than any cry of pain,
That might escape the lips of one who dies.
Doth his heart fail him? Doth he fall away
In the last hour from God? O Sirion, Sirion,
Art thou afraid? I do not hear thy voice.
Die as thy brothers died. Thou must not live!

SCENE II. THE MOTHER; ANTIOCHUS; SIRION.

THE MOTHER.

Are they all dead?

ANTIOCHUS.

     Of all thy Seven Sons
One only lives. Behold them where they lie;
How dost thou like this picture?

THE MOTHER.

       God in heaven!
Can a man do such deeds, and yet not die
By the recoil of his own wickedness?
Ye murdered, bleeding, mutilated bodies
That were my children once, and still are mine,
I cannot watch o'er you as Rispah watched
In sackcloth o'er the seven sons of Saul,
Till water drop upon you out of heaven
And wash this blood away! I cannot mourn
As she, the daughter of Aiah, mourned the dead,
From the beginning of the barley-harvest

Until the autumn rains, and suffered not
The birds of air to rest on them by day,
Nor the wild beasts by night. For ye have died
A better death, a death so full of life
That I ought rather to rejoice than mourn.—
Wherefore art thou not dead, O Sirion?
Wherefore art thou the only living thing
Among thy brothers dead? Art thou afraid?

    ANTIOCHUS.

O woman, I have spared him for thy sake,
For he is fair to look upon and comely;
And I have sworn to him by all the gods
That I would crown his life with joy and honor,
Heap treasures on him, luxuries, delights,
Make him my friend and keeper of my secrets,
If he would turn from your Mosaic Law
And be as we are; but he will not listen.

    THE MOTHER.

My noble Sirion!

    ANTIOCHUS.

    Therefore I beseech thee,

Who art his mother, thou wouldst speak with him,
And wouldst persuade him. I am sick of blood.

     THE MOTHER.

Yea, I will speak with him and will persuade him.
O Sirion, my son! have pity on me,
On me that bare thee, and that gave thee suck,
And fed and nourished thee, and brought thee up
With the dear trouble of a mother's care
Unto this age. Look on the heavens above thee,
And on the earth and all that is therein;
Consider that God made them out of things
That were not; and that likewise in this manner
Mankind was made. Then fear not this tormentor;
But, being worthy of thy brethren, take
Thy death as they did, that I may receive thee
Again in mercy with them.

     ANTIOCHUS.

       I am mocked,
Yea, I am laughed to scorn.

     SIRION.

       Whom wait ye for?

Never will I obey the King's commandment,
But the commandment of the ancient Law,
That was by Moses given unto our fathers.
And thou, O godless man, that of all others
Art the most wicked, be not lifted up,
Nor puffed up with uncertain hopes, uplifting
Thy hand against the servants of the Lord,
For thou hast not escaped the righteous judgment
Of the Almighty God, who seeth all things!

ANTIOCHUS.

He is no God of mine; I fear him not.

SIRION.

My brothers, who have suffered a brief pain,
Are dead; but thou, Antiochus, shalt suffer
The punishment of pride. I offer up
My body and my life, beseeching God
That he would speedily be merciful
Unto our nation, and that thou by plagues
Mysterious and by torments mayest confess
That he alone is God.

ANTIOCHUS.

            Ye both shall perish
By torments worse than any that your God,
Here or hereafter, hath in store for me.

THE MOTHER.

My Sirion, I am proud of thee!

ANTIOCHUS.

                    Be silent!
Go to thy bed of torture in yon chamber,
Where lie so many sleepers, heartless mother!
Thy footsteps will not wake them, nor thy voice,
Nor wilt thou hear, amid thy troubled dreams,
Thy children crying for thee in the night!

THE MOTHER.

O Death, that stretchest thy white hands to me,
I fear them not, but press them to my lips,
That are as white as thine; for I am Death,
Nay, am the Mother of Death, seeing these sons
All lying lifeless.—Kiss me, Sirion.

ACT III.

The Battle-field of Beth-horon.

SCENE I. JUDAS MACCABÆUS *in armor before his tent.*

JUDAS.

THE trumpets sound; the echoes of the mountains
Answer them, as the Sabbath morning breaks
Over Beth-horon and its battle-field,
Where the great captain of the hosts of God,
A slave brought up in the brick-fields of Egypt,
O'ercame the Amorites. There was no day
Like that, before or after it, nor shall be.
The sun stood still; the hammers of the hail
Beat on their harness; and the captains set
Their weary feet upon the necks of kings,
As I will upon thine, Antiochus,
Thou man of blood! — Behold the rising sun
Strikes on the golden letters of my banner,
Be Elohim Yehovah! Who is like
To thee, O Lord, among the gods?—Alas!

I am not Joshua, I cannot say,
"Sun, stand thou still on Gibeon; and thou Moon,
In Ajalon!" Nor am I one who wastes
The fateful time in useless lamentation;
But one who bears his life upon his hand
To lose it or to save it, as may best
Serve the designs of Him who giveth life.

SCENE II. JUDAS MACCABÆUS; JEWISH FUGITIVES.

JUDAS.

Who and what are ye, that with furtive steps
Steal in among our tents?

FUGITIVES.

O Maccabæus,
Outcasts are we, and fugitives as thou art,
Jews of Jerusalem, that have escaped
From the polluted city, and from death.

JUDAS.

None can escape from death. Say that ye come
To die for Israel, and ye are welcome.
What tidings bring ye?

####### FUGITIVES.

Tidings of despair.
The Temple is laid waste; the precious vessels,
Censers of gold, vials and veils and crowns,
And golden ornaments, and hidden treasures,
Have all been taken from it, and the Gentiles
With revelling and with riot fill its courts,
And dally with harlots in the holy places.

####### JUDAS.

All this I knew before.

####### FUGITIVES.

Upon the altar
Are things profane, things by the law forbidden;
Nor can we keep our Sabbaths or our Feasts,
But on the festivals of Dionysus
Must walk in their processions, bearing ivy
To crown a drunken god.

####### JUDAS.

This too I know.
But tell me of the Jews. How fare the Jews?

FUGITIVES.

The coming of this mischief hath been sore
And grievous to the people. All the land
Is full of lamentation and of mourning.
The Princes and the Elders weep and wail;
The young men and the maidens are made feeble;
The beauty of the women hath been changed.

JUDAS.

And are there none to die for Israel?
'Tis not enough to mourn. Breastplate and harness
Are better things than sackcloth. Let the women
Lament for Israel; the men should die.

FUGITIVES.

Both men and women die; old men and young:
Old Eleazer died; and Máhala
With all her Seven Sons.

JUDAS.

Antiochus,
At every step thou takest there is left
A bloody footprint in the street, by which
The avenging wrath of God will track thee out!

It is enough. Go to the sutler's tents:
Those of you who are men, put on such armor
As ye may find; those of you who are women,
Buckle that armor on; and for a watchword
Whisper, or cry aloud, "The Help of God."

SCENE III. JUDAS MACCABÆUS; NICANOR.

NICANOR.

Hail, Judas Maccabæus!

JUDAS.

Hail!—Who art thou
That comest here in this mysterious guise
Into our camp unheralded?

NICANOR.

A herald
Sent from Nicanor.

JUDAS.

Heralds come not thus.
Armed with thy shirt of mail from head to heel,
Thou glidest like a serpent silently
Into my presence. Wherefore dost thou turn

Thy face from me! A herald speaks his errand
With forehead unabashed. Thou art a spy
Sent by Nicanor.

                NICANOR.
                    No disguise avails!
Behold my face; I am Nicanor's self.

                JUDAS.
Thou art indeed Nicanor. I salute thee.
What brings thee hither to this hostile camp
Thus unattended?

                NICANOR.
                    Confidence in thee.
Thou hast the nobler virtues of thy race,
Without the failings that attend those virtues.
Thou canst be strong, and yet not tyrannous,
Canst righteous be and not intolerant.
Let there be peace between us.

                JUDAS.
                        What is peace?
Is it to bow in silence to our victors?
Is it to see our cities sacked and pillaged,

Our people slain, or sold as slaves, or fleeing
At night-time by the blaze of burning towns;
Jerusalem laid waste; the Holy Temple
Polluted with strange gods? Are these things peace?

NICANOR.

These are the dire necessities that wait
On war, whose loud and bloody enginery
I seek to stay. Let there be peace between
Antiochus and thee.

JUDAS.

Antiochus?
What is Antiochus, that he should prate
Of peace to me, who am a fugitive?
To-day he shall be lifted up; to-morrow
Shall not be found, because he is returned
Unto his dust; his thought has come to nothing.
There is no peace between us, nor can be,
Until this banner floats upon the walls
Of our Jerusalem.

NICANOR.

Between that city

And thee there lies a waving wall of tents,
Held by a host of forty thousand foot,
And horsemen seven thousand.   What hast thou
To bring against all these?

    JUDAS.

      The power of God,
Whose breath shall scatter your white tents abroad,
As flakes of snow.

    NICANOR.

     Your Mighty One in heaven
Will not do battle on the Seventh Day;
It is his day of rest.

    JUDAS.

    Silence, blasphemer.
Go to thy tents.

    NICANOR.

   Shall it be war or peace?

    JUDAS.

War, war, and only war.   Go to thy tents
That shall be scattered, as by you were scattered

The torn and trampled pages of the Law,
Blown through the windy streets.

NICANOR.
       Farewell, brave foe!

JUDAS.
Ho, there, my captains! Have safe-conduct given
Unto Nicanor's herald through the camp,
And come yourselves to me.—Farewell, Nicanor!

SCENE IV. JUDAS MACCABÆUS; CAPTAINS AND SOLDIERS.

JUDAS.
The hour is come. Gather the host together
For battle. Lo, with trumpets and with songs
The army of Nicanor comes against us.
Go forth to meet them, praying in your hearts,
And fighting with your hands.

CAPTAINS.
       Look forth and see!
The morning sun is shining on their shields
Of gold and brass; the mountains glisten with them,

And shine like lamps. And we who are so few
And poorly armed, and ready to faint with fasting,
How shall we fight against this multitude?

JUDAS.

The victory of a battle standeth not
In multitudes, but in the strength that cometh
From heaven above. The Lord forbid that I
Should do this thing, and flee away from them.
Nay, if our hour be come, then let us die;
Let us not stain our honor.

CAPTAINS.

      'Tis the Sabbath.
Wilt thou fight on the Sabbath, Maccabæus?

JUDAS.

Ay; when I fight the battles of the Lord,
I fight them on his day, as on all others.
Have ye forgotten certain fugitives
That fled once to these hills, and hid themselves
In caves? How their pursuers camped against them
Upon the Seventh Day, and challenged them?
And how they answered not, nor cast a stone,

Nor stopped the places where they lay concealed,
But meekly perished with their wives and children,
Even to the number of a thousand souls!
We who are fighting for our laws and lives
Will not so perish.

    CAPTAINS.

        Lead us to the battle!

    JUDAS.

And let our watchword be, "The Help of God!"
Last night I dreamed a dream; and in my vision
Beheld Onias, our High-Priest of old,
Who holding up his hands prayed for the Jews.
This done, in the like manner there appeared
An old man, and exceeding glorious,
With hoary hair, and of a wonderful
And excellent majesty. And Onias said:
"This is a lover of the Jews, who prayeth
Much for the people and the Holy City,—
God's prophet Jeremias." And the prophet
Held forth his right hand and gave unto me
A sword of gold; and giving it he said:

"Take thou this holy sword, a gift from God,
And with it thou shalt wound thine adversaries."

CAPTAINS.

The Lord is with us!

JUDAS.

Hark! I hear the trumpets
Sound from Beth-horon; from the battle-field
Of Joshua, where he smote the Amorites,
Smote the Five Kings of Eglon and of Jarmuth,
Of Hebron, Lachish, and Jerusalem,
As we to-day will smite Nicanor's hosts,
And leave a memory of great deeds behind us.

CAPTAINS AND SOLDIERS.

The Help of God!

JUDAS.

Be Elohim Yehovah!
Lord, thou didst send thine Angel in the time
Of Ezekias, King of Israel,
And in the armies of Sennacherib
Didst slay a hundred fourscore and five thousand.
Wherefore, O Lord of heaven, now also send

Before us a good angel for a fear,
And through the might of thy right arm, let those
Be stricken with terror that have come this day
Against thy holy people to blaspheme!

ACT IV.

The outer Courts of the Temple at Jerusalem.

SCENE I. JUDAS MACCABÆUS; CAPTAINS; JEWS.

JUDAS.

BEHOLD, our enemies are discomfited.
Jerusalem is fallen; and our banners
Float from her battlements, and o'er her gates
Nicanor's severed head, a sign of terror,
Blackens in wind and sun.

CAPTAINS.

　　　　　　　O Maccabæus,
The citadel of Antiochus, wherein
The Mother with her Seven Sons was murdered,
Is still defiant.

JUDAS.
Wait.

CAPTAINS.
Its hateful aspect
Insults us with the bitter memories
Of other days.

JUDAS.
Wait; it shall disappear
And vanish as a cloud. First let us cleanse
The Sanctuary. See, it is become
Waste like a wilderness. Its golden gates
Wrenched from their hinges and consumed by fire;
Shrubs growing in its courts as in a forest;
Upon its altars hideous and strange idols;
And strewn about its pavement at my feet
Its Sacred Books, half burned and painted o'er
With images of heathen gods.

JEWS.
Woe! woe!
Our beauty and our glory are laid waste!
The Gentiles have profaned our holy places!

Lamentation and alarm of trumpets.

JUDAS.

This sound of trumpets, and this lamentation,
The heart-cry of a people toward the heavens,
Stir me to wrath and vengeance. Go, my captains;
I hold you back no longer. Batter down
The citadel of Antiochus, while here
We sweep away his altars and his gods.

SCENE II. JUDAS MACCABÆUS; JASON; JEWS.

JEWS.

Lurking among the ruins of the Temple,
Deep in its inner courts, we found this man,
Clad as High-Priest.

JUDAS.

                    I ask not who thou art.
I know thy face, writ over with deceit
As are these tattered volumes of the Law
With heathen images. A priest of God
Wast thou in other days, but thou art now
A priest of Satan. Traitor, thou art Jason.

JASON.

I am thy prisoner, Judas Maccabæus,
And it would ill become me to conceal
My name or office.

JUDAS.

    Over yonder gate
There hangs the head of one who was a Greek.
What should prevent me now, thou man of sin,
From hanging at its side the head of one
Who born a Jew hath made himself a Greek?

JASON.

Justice prevents thee.

JUDAS.

    Justice? Thou art stained
With every crime 'gainst which the Decalogue
Thunders with all its thunder.

JASON.

    If not Justice,
Then Mercy, her handmaiden.

JUDAS.

    When hast thou

At any time, to any man or woman,
Or even to any little child, shown mercy?

JASON.

I have but done what King Antiochus
Commanded me.

JUDAS.

True, thou hast been the weapon
With which he struck; but hast been such a weapon,
So flexible, so fitted to his hand .
It tempted him to strike. So thou hast urged him
To double wickedness, thine own and his.
Where is this King? Is he in Antioch
Among his women still, and from his windows
Throwing down gold by handfuls, for the rabble
To scramble for?

JASON.

Nay, he is gone from there,
Gone with an army into the far East.

JUDAS.

And wherefore gone?

JASON.
       I know not.   For the space
Of forty days almost were horsemen seen
Running in air, in cloth of gold, and armed
With lances, like a band of soldiery;
It was a sign of triumph.
             JUDAS.
                   Or of death.
Wherefore art thou not with him?
             JASON.
                      I was left
For service in the Temple.
             JUDAS.
                   To pollute it,
And to corrupt the Jews; for there are men
Whose presence is corruption; to be with them
Degrades us and deforms the things we do.
             JASON.
I never made a boast, as some men do,
Of my superior virtue, nor denied
The weakness of my nature, that hath made me
Subservient to the will of other men.

JUDAS.

Upon this day, the five-and-twentieth day
Of the month Caslan, was the Temple here
Profaned by strangers,—by Antiochus
And thee, his instrument. Upon this day
Shall it be cleansed. Thou, who didst lend thyself
Unto this profanation, canst not be
A witness of these solemn services.
There can be nothing clean where thou art present.
The people put to death Callisthenes,
Who burned the Temple gates; and if they find thee
Will surely slay thee. I will spare thy life
To punish thee the longer. Thou shalt wander
Among strange nations. Thou, that hast cast out
So many from their native land, shalt perish
In a strange land. Thou, that hast left so many
Unburied, shalt have none to mourn for thee,
Nor any solemn funerals at all,
Nor sepulchre with thy fathers.—Get thee hence!

Music. Procession of Priests and people, with citherns, harps and cymbals. JUDAS MACCABÆUS *puts himself at their head, and they go into the inner courts.*

SCENE III. JASON, *alone.*

JASON.

Through the Gate Beautiful I see them come
With branches and green boughs and leaves of palm,
And pass into the inner courts. Alas!
I should be with them, should be one of them,
But in an evil hour, an hour of weakness,
That cometh unto all, I fell away
From the old faith, and did not clutch the new,
Only an outward semblance of belief;
For the new faith I cannot make mine own,
Not being born to it. It hath no root
Within me. I am neither Jew nor Greek,
But stand between them both, a renegade
To each in turn; having no longer faith
In gods or men. Then what mysterious charm,
What fascination is it chains my feet,
And keeps me gazing like a curious child
Into the holy places, where the priests
Have raised their altar? — Striking stones together,

They take fire out of them, and light the lamps
In the great candlestick.   They spread the veils,
And set the loaves of showbread on the table.
The incense burns; the well-remembered odor
Comes wafted unto me, and takes me back
To other days. I see myself among them
As I was then; and the old superstition
Creeps over me again!—A childish fancy!—
And hark! they sing with citherns and with cymbals,
And all the people fall upon their faces,
Praying and worshipping!—I will away
Into the East, to meet Antiochus
Upon his homeward journey, crowned with triumph.
Alas! to-day I would give everything
To see a friend's face, or to hear a voice
That had the slightest tone of comfort in it!

ACT V.

The Mountains of Ecbatana.

SCENE I. ANTIOCHUS; PHILIP; ATTENDANTS.

ANTIOCHUS.

HERE let us rest awhile. Where are we, Philip?
What place is this?

PHILIP.

My Lord, these are the mountains
Of Ecbatana. These are the Orontes.

ANTIOCHUS.

The Orontes is my river at Antioch.
Why did I leave it? Why have I been tempted
By coverings of gold and shields and breastplates
To plunder Elymais, and be driven
From out its gates, as by a fiery blast
Out of a furnace?

PHILIP.

These are fortune's changes.

ANTIOCHUS.

What a defeat it was! The Persian horsemen
Came like a mighty wind, the wind Khamáseen,
And melted us away, and scattered us
As if we were dead leaves, or desert sand.

PHILIP.

Be comforted, my Lord; for thou hast lost
But what thou hadst not.

ANTIOCHUS.

              I, who made the Jews
Skip like the grasshoppers, am made myself
To skip among these stones.

PHILIP.

                  Be not discouraged.
Thy realm of Syria remains to thee;
That is not lost nor marred.

ANTIOCHUS.

              O, where are now
The splendors of my court, my baths and banquets?
Where are my players and my dancing women?
Where are my sweet musicians with their pipes,

That made me merry in the olden time?
I am a laughing-stock to man and brute.
The very camels, with their ugly faces,
Mock me and laugh at me.

PHILIP.

                Alas! my Lord,
It is not so. If thou wouldst sleep awhile,
All would be well.

ANTIOCHUS.

                Sleep from mine eyes is gone,
And my heart faileth me for very care.
Dost thou remember, Philip, the old fable
Told us when we were boys, in which the bear
Going for honey overturns the hive,
And is stung blind by bees? I am that beast,
Stung by the Persian swarms of Elymais.

PHILIP.

When thou art come again to Antioch
These thoughts will be as covered and forgotten
As are the tracks of Pharaoh's chariot-wheels
In the Egyptian sands.

ANTIOCHUS.

          Ah! when I come
Again to Antioch! When will that be?
Alas! alas!

SCENE II. ANTIOCHUS; PHILIP; A MESSENGER.

MESSENGER.

May the King live forever!

ANTIOCHUS.

Who art thou, and whence comest thou?

MESSENGER.

                My Lord,
I am a messenger from Antioch,
Sent here by Lysias.

ANTIOCHUS.

          A strange foreboding
Of something evil overshadows me.
I am no reader of the Jewish Scriptures;
I know not Hebrew; but my High-Priest Jason,
As I remember, told me of a Prophet

Who saw a little cloud rise from the sea
Like a man's hand, and soon the heaven was black
With clouds and rain. Here, Philip, read; I cannot;
I see that cloud. It makes the letters dim
Before mine eyes.

   PHILIP, *reading.*

   "To King Antiochus,
The God, Epiphanes."

   ANTIOCHUS.

   O mockery!
Even Lysias laughs at me!—Go on, go on!

   PHILIP, *reading.*

"We pray thee hasten thy return. The realm
Is falling from thee. Since thou hast gone from us
The victories of Judas Maccabæus
Form all our annals. First he overthrew
Thy forces at Beth-horon, and passed on,
And took Jerusalem, the Holy City.
And then Emmaus fell; and then Bethsura;
Ephron and all the towns of Galaad,
And Maccabæus marched to Carnion."

ANTIOCHUS.

Enough, enough! Go call my chariot-men;
We will drive forward, forward without ceasing,
Until we come to Antioch. My captains,
My Lysias, Gorgias, Seron, and Nicanor,
Are babes in battle, and this dreadful Jew
Will rob me of my kingdom and my crown.
My elephants shall trample him to dust;
I will wipe out his nation, and will make
Jerusalem a common burying-place,
And every home within its walls a tomb!

Throws up his hands, and sinks into the arms of attendants, who lay him upon a bank.

PHILIP.

Antiochus! Antiochus! Alas,
The King is ill! What is it, O my Lord?

ANTIOCHUS.

Nothing. A sudden and sharp spasm of pain,
As if the lightning struck me, or the knife
Of an assassin smote me to the heart.
'Tis passed, even as it came. Let us set forward.

PHILIP.

See that the chariots be in readiness;
We will depart forthwith.

ANTIOCHUS.

A moment more.
I cannot stand. I am become at once
Weak as an infant. Ye will have to lead me.
Jove, or Jehovah, or whatever name
Thou wouldst be named,—it is alike to me,—
If I knew how to pray, I would entreat
To live a little longer.

PHILIP.

O my Lord,
Thou shalt not die; we will not let thee die!

ANTIOCHUS.

How canst thou help it, Philip? O the pain!
Stab after stab. Thou hast no shield against
This unseen weapon. God of Israel,
Since all the other gods abandon me,
Help me. I will release the Holy City,
Garnish with goodly gifts the Holy Temple.

Thy people, whom I judged to be unworthy
To be so much as buried, shall be equal
Unto the citizens of Antioch.
I will become a Jew, and will declare
Through all the world that is inhabited
The power of God!

    PHILIP.

      He faints. It is like death.
Bring here the royal litter. We will bear him
Into the camp, while yet he lives.

    ANTIOCHUS.

        O Philip,
Into what tribulation am I come!
Alas! I now remember all the evil
That I have done the Jews; and for this cause
These troubles are upon me, and behold
I perish through great grief in a strange land.

    PHILIP.
Antiochus! my King!

    ANTIOCHUS.

     Nay, King no longer.

Take thou my royal robes, my signet-ring,
My crown and sceptre, and deliver them
Unto my son, Antiochus Eupator;
And unto the good Jews, my citizens,
In all my towns, say that their dying monarch
Wisheth them joy, prosperity, and health.
I who, puffed up with pride and arrogance,
Thought all the kingdoms of the earth mine own,
If I would but outstretch my hand and take them,
Meet face to face a greater potentate,
King Death—Epiphanes—the Illustrious!

Dies.

BOOK THIRD.

A HANDFUL OF TRANSLATIONS.

THE FUGITIVE.

Tartar Song, from the Prose Version of Chodzko.

I.

"HE is gone to the desert land!
I can see the shining mane
Of his horse on the distant plain,
As he rides with his Kossak band!

"Come back, rebellious one!
Let thy proud heart relent;
Come back to my tall, white tent,
Come back, my only son!

"Thy hand in freedom shall
Cast thy hawks, when morning breaks,
On the swans of the Seven Lakes,
On the lakes of Karajal.

"I will give thee leave to stray
And pasture thy hunting steeds
In the long grass and the reeds
Of the meadows of Karaday.

"I will give thee my coat of mail,
Of softest leather made,
With choicest steel inlaid;
Will not all this prevail?"

II.

"This hand no longer shall
Cast my hawks, when morning breaks,
On the swans of the Seven Lakes,
On the lakes of Karajal.

"I will no longer stray
And pasture my hunting steeds
In the long grass and the reeds
Of the meadows of Karaday.

"Though thou give me thy coat of mail,
Of softest leather made,
With choicest steel inlaid,
All this cannot prevail.

"What right hast thou, O Khan,
To me, who am mine own,
Who am slave to God alone,
And not to any man?

"God will appoint the day
When I again shall be
By the blue, shallow sea,
Where the steel-bright sturgeons play.

"God, who doth care for me,
In the barren wilderness,
On unknown hills, no less
Will my companion be.

"When I wander lonely and lost
In the wind; when I watch at night

Like a hungry wolf, and am white
And covered with hoar-frost;

"Yea, wheresoever I be,
In the yellow desert sands,
In mountains or unknown lands,
Allah will care for me!"

III.

Then Sobra, the old, old man,—
Three hundred and sixty years
Had he lived in this land of tears,
Bowed down and said, "O Khan!

"If you bid me, I will speak.
There's no sap in dry grass,
No marrow in dry bones! Alas,
The mind of old men is weak!

"I am old, I am very old:
I have seen the primeval man,
I have seen the great Gengis Khan,
Arrayed in his robes of gold.

"What I say to you is the truth;
And I say to you, O Khan,
Pursue not the star-white man,
Pursue not the beautiful youth.

"Him the Almighty made,
And brought him forth of the light,
At the verge and end of the night,
When men on the mountain prayed.

" He was born at the break of day,
When abroad the angels walk;
He hath listened to their talk,
And he knoweth what they say.

"Gifted with Allah's grace,
Like the moon of Ramazan

When it shines in the skies, O Khan,
Is the light of his beautiful face.

"When first on earth he trod,
The first words that he said
Were these, as he stood and prayed,
There is no God but God!

"And he shall be king of men,
For Allah hath heard his prayer,
And the Archangel in the air,
Gabriel, hath said, Amen!"

THE SIEGE OF KAZAN.

Tartar Song, from the Prose Version of Chodzko.

BLACK are the moors before Kazan,
    And their stagnant waters smell of blood:
I said in my heart, with horse and man,
    I will swim across this shallow flood.

Under the feet of Argamack,
    Like new moons were the shoes he bare,
Silken trappings hung on his back,
    In a talisman on his neck, a prayer.

My warriors, thought I, are following me;
    But when I looked behind, alas!
Not one of all the band could I see,
    All had sunk in the black morass!

Where are our shallow fords? and where
    The power of Kazan with its fourfold gates?
From the prison windows our maidens fair
    Talk of us still through the iron grates.

We cannot hear them; for horse and man
    Lie buried deep in the dark abyss!
Ah! the black day hath come down on Kazan!
    Ah! was ever a grief like this?

THE BOY AND THE BROOK.

Armenian Popular Song, from the Prose Version of Alishan.

Down from yon distant mountain height
   The brooklet flows through the village street;
A boy comes forth to wash his hands,
Washing, yes washing, there he stands,
   In the water cool and sweet.

Brook, from what mountain dost thou come
   O my brooklet cool and sweet!
I come from yon mountain high and cold,
Where lieth the new snow on the old,
   And melts in the summer heat.

Brook, to what river dost thou go?
   O my brooklet cool and sweet!

I go to the river there below
Where in bunches the violets grow,
   And sun and shadow meet.

Brook, to what garden dost thou go?
   O my brooklet cool and sweet!
I go to the garden in the vale
Where all night long the nightingale
   Her love-song doth repeat.

Brook, to what fountain dost thou go?
   O my brooklet cool and sweet!
I go to the fountain at whose brink
The maid that loves thee comes to drink,
And whenever she looks therein,
I rise to meet her, and kiss her chin,
   And my joy is then complete.

TO THE STORK.

Armenian Popular Song, from the Prose Version of Alishan.

WELCOME, O Stork! that dost wing
　Thy flight from the far-away!
Thou hast brought us the signs of Spring,
　Thou hast made our sad hearts gay.

Descend, O Stork! descend
　Upon our roof to rest;
In our ash-tree, O my friend,
　My darling, make thy nest.

To thee, O Stork, I complain,
　O Stork, to thee I impart
The thousand sorrows, the pain
　And aching of my heart.

When thou away didst go,
    Away from this tree of ours,
The withering winds did blow,
    And dried up all the flowers.

Dark grew the brilliant sky,
    Cloudy and dark and drear;
They were breaking the snow on high,
    And winter was drawing near.

From Varaca's rocky wall,
    From the rock of Varaca unrolled,
The snow came and covered all,
    And the green meadow was cold.

O Stork, our garden with snow
    Was hidden away and lost,
And the rose-trees that in it grow
    Were withered by snow and frost.

CONSOLATION.

To M. Duperrier, Gentleman of Aix in Provence, on the Death of his Daughter.

FROM MALHERBE.

WILL then, Duperrier, thy sorrow be eternal?
    And shall the sad discourse
Whispered within thy heart, by tenderness paternal,
    Only augment its force?

Thy daughter's mournful fate, into the tomb descending
    By death's frequented ways,
Has it become to thee a labyrinth never ending,
    Where thy lost reason strays?

I know the charms that made her youth a benediction:
    Nor should I be content,

As a censorious friend, to solace thine affliction,
    By her disparagement.

But she was of the world, which fairest things exposes
    To fates the most forlorn;
A rose, she too hath lived as long as live the roses,
    The space of one brief morn.

   *   *   *   *   *

Death has his rigorous laws, unparalleled, unfeeling;
    All prayers to him are vain;
Cruel, he stops his ears, and, deaf to our appealing,
    He leaves us to complain.

The poor man in his hut, with only thatch for cover,
    Unto these laws must bend;
The sentinel that guards the barriers of the Louvre
    Cannot our kings defend,

To murmur against death, in petulant defiance,
    Is never for the best;
To will what God doth will, that is the only science
    That gives us any rest.

TO CARDINAL RICHELIEU.

FROM MALHERBE.

Thou mighty Prince of Church and State,
Richelieu! until the hour of death,
Whatever road man chooses, Fate
Still holds him subject to her breath.
Spun of all silks, our days and nights
Have sorrows woven with delights;
And of this intermingled shade
Our various destiny appears,
Even as one sees the course of years
Of summers and of winters made.

Sometimes the soft, deceitful hours
Let us enjoy the halcyon wave;
Sometimes impending peril lowers
Beyond the seaman's skill to save.

The Wisdom, infinitely wise,
That gives to human destinies
Their foreordained necessity,
Has made no law more fixed below,
Than the alternate ebb and flow
Of Fortune and Adversity.

THE ANGEL AND THE CHILD.

FROM JEAN REBOUL, THE BAKER OF NISMES.

An angel with a radiant face,
   Above a cradle bent to look,
Seemed his own image there to trace,
   As in the waters of a brook.

"Dear child! who me resemblest so,"
   It whispered, "come, O come with me!
Happy together let us go,
   The earth unworthy is of thee!

"Here none to perfect bliss attain;
   The soul in pleasure suffering lies;
Joy hath an undertone of pain,
   And even the happiest hours their sighs.

"Fear doth at every portal knock;
　　Never a day serene and pure
From the o'ershadowing tempest's shock
　　Hath made the morrow's dawn secure.

"What, then, shall sorrows and shall fears
　　Come to disturb so pure a brow?
And with the bitterness of tears
　　These eyes of azure troubled grow?

"Ah no! into the fields of space,
　　Away shalt thou escape with me;
And Providence will grant thee grace
　　Of all the days that were to be.

"Let no one in thy dwelling cower,
　　In sombre vestments draped and veiled;
But let them welcome thy last hour,
　　As thy first moments once they hailed.

"Without a cloud be there each brow;
　　There let the grave no shadow cast;

When one is pure as thou art now,
   The fairest day is still the last."

And waving wide his wings of white,
   The angel, at these words, had sped
'Towards the eternal realms of light!—
   Poor mother! see, thy son is dead!

TO ITALY.

FROM FILICAJA.

Italy! Italy! thou who 'rt doomed to wear
    The fatal gift of beauty, and possess
    The dower funest of infinite wretchedness,
    Written upon thy forehead by despair;
Ah! would that thou wert stronger, or less fair,
    That they might fear thee more, or love thee less,
    Who in the splendor of thy loveliness
    Seem wasting, yet to mortal combat dare!
Then from the Alps I should not see descending
    Such torrents of armed men, nor Gallic horde
    Drinking the wave of Po, distained with gore,
Nor should I see thee girded with a sword
    Not thine, and with the stranger's arm contending,
    Victor or vanquished, slave forevermore.

WANDERER'S NIGHT-SONGS.

FROM GOETHE.

I.

THOU that from the heavens art,
Every pain and sorrow stillest,
And the doubly wretched heart
Doubly with refreshment fillest,
I am weary with contending!
Why this rapture and unrest?
Peace descending
Come, ah, come into my breast!

II.

O'er all the hill-tops
Is quiet now,
In all the tree-tops
Hearest thou

Hardly a breath;
The birds are asleep in the trees:
Wait; soon like these
Thou too shalt rest.

REMORSE.

FROM AUGUST VON PLATEN.

How I started up in the night, in the night,
  Drawn on without rest or reprieval!
The streets, with their watchmen, were lost to my
    sight,
  As I wandered so light
  In the night, in the night,
Through the gate with the arch mediæval.

The mill-brook rushed from the rocky height,
  I leaned o'er the bridge in my yearning;
Deep under me watched I the waves in their flight,
  As they glided so light
  In the night, in the night,
Yet backward not one was returning.

O'erhead were revolving, so countless and bright,
    The stars in melodious existence;
And with them the moon, more serenely bedight;—
    They sparkled so light
    In the night, in the night,
Through the magical, measureless distance.

And upward I gazed in the night, in the night,
    And again on the waves in their fleeting;
Ah woe! thou hast wasted thy days in delight,
    Now silence thou light,
    In the night, in the night,
The remorse in thy heart that is beating.

SANTA TERESA'S BOOK-MARK.

FROM THE SPANISH OF SANTA TERESA.

Let nothing disturb thee,
Nothing affright thee;
All things are passing;
God never changeth;
Patient endurance
Attaineth to all things;
Who God possesseth
In nothing is wanting;
Alone God sufficeth.

INTERLUDE AND FINALE OF CHRISTUS.

I.

THE ABBOT JOACHIM.

A room in the Convent of Flora in Calabria. Night.

JOACHIM.

The wind is rising; it seizes and shakes
The doors and window-blinds, and makes
Mysterious moanings in the halls;
The convent-chimneys seem almost
The trumpets of some heavenly host,
Setting its watch upon our walls!
Where it listeth, there it bloweth;
We hear the sound, but no man knoweth
Whence it cometh or whither it goeth,
And thus it is with the Holy Ghost.
O breath of God! O my delight
In many a vigil of the night,

Like the great voice in Patmos heard
By John, the Evangelist of the Word,
I hear thee behind me saying: Write
In a book the things that thou hast seen,
The things that are, and that have been,
And the things that shall hereafter be!

This convent, on the rocky crest
Of the Calabrian hills, to me
A Patmos is wherein I rest;
While round about me like a sea
The white mists roll, and overflow
The world that lies unseen below
In darkness and in mystery.
Here in the Spirit, in the vast
Embrace of God's encircling arm,
Am I uplifted from all harm;
The world seems something far away,
Something belonging to the Past,
A hostlery, a peasant's farm,
That lodged me for a night or day,

In which I care not to remain,
Nor having left, to see again.

Thus, in the hollow of God's hand
I dwelt on sacred Tabor's height,
When as a simple acolyte
I journeyed to the Holy Land,
A pilgrim for my Master's sake,
And saw the Galilean Lake,
And walked through many a village street
That once had echoed to his feet.
There first I heard the great command,
The voice behind me saying: Write!
And suddenly my soul became
Illumined by a flash of flame,
That left imprinted on my thought
The image I in vain had sought,
And which forever shall remain;
As sometimes from these windows high,
Gazing at midnight on the sky
Black with a storm of wind and rain,

I have beheld a sudden glare
Of lightning lay the landscape bare,
With tower and town and hill and plain
Distinct, and burnt into my brain,
Never to be effaced again!

And I have written. These volumes three,
The Apocalypse, the Harmony
Of the Sacred Scriptures, new and old,
And the Psalter with Ten Strings, enfold
Within their pages, all and each,
The Eternal Gospel that I teach.
Well I remember the Kingdom of Heaven
Hath been likened to a little leaven
Hidden in two measures of meal,
Until it leavened the whole mass;
So likewise will it come to pass
With the doctrine that I here conceal.

Open and manifest to me
The truth appears, and must be told;
All sacred mysteries are threefold;

Three Persons in the Trinity,
Three Ages of Humanity,
And Holy Scriptures likewise Three,
Of Fear, of Wisdom, and of Love;
For Wisdom that begins in Fear
Endeth in Love; the atmosphere
In which the soul delights to be,
And finds that perfect liberty,
Which cometh only from above.

In the first Age, the early prime
And dawn of all historic time,
The Father reigned; and face to face
He spake with the primeval race.
Bright Angels, on his errands sent,
Sat with the patriarch in his tent;
His prophets thundered in the street;
His lightnings flashed, his hail-storms beat;
In tempest and in cloud he came,
In earthquake and in flood and flame!

The fear of God is in his Book;
The pages of the Pentateuch
Are full of the terror of his name.

Then reigned the Son; his Covenant
Was peace on earth, good-will to man;
With him the reign of Law began.
He was the Wisdom and the Word,
And sent his Angels Ministrant,
Unterrified and undeterred
To rescue souls forlorn and lost,
The troubled, tempted, tempest-tost,
To heal, to comfort, and to teach.
The fiery tongues of Pentecost
His symbols were, that they should preach
In every form of human speech,
From continent to continent.
He is the Light Divine, whose rays
Across the thousand years unspent
Shine through the darkness of our days,

And touch with their celestial fires
Our churches and our convent spires.
His Book is the New Testament.

These Ages now are of the Past;
And the Third Age begins at last.
The coming of the Holy Ghost,
The reign of Grace, the reign of Love
Brightens the mountain-tops above,
And the dark outline of the coast.
Already the whole land is white
With convent walls, as if by night
A snow had fallen on hill and height!
Already from the streets and marts
Of town and traffic, and low cares,
Men climb the consecrated stairs
With weary feet, and bleeding hearts;
And leave the world, and its delights,
Its passions, struggles, and despairs,
For contemplation and for prayers
In cloister-cells of Cœnobites.

Eternal benedictions rest
Upon thy name, Saint Benedict!
Founder of convents in the West,
Who built on Mount Cassino's crest
In the Land of Labor, thine eagle's nest!
May I be found not derelict
In aught of faith or godly fear,
If I have written, in many a page,
The Gospel of the coming age,
The Eternal Gospel men shall hear.
O may I live resembling thee,
And die at last as thou hast died;
So that hereafter men may see,
Within the choir, a form of air,
Standing with arms outstretched in prayer,
As one that hath been crucified!

My work is finished; I am strong
In faith and hope and charity;
For I have written the things I see,
The things that have been and shall be,

Conscious of right, nor fearing wrong;
Because I am in love with Love,
And the sole thing I hate is Hate;
For Hate is death; and Love is life,
A peace, a splendor from above;
And Hate, a never-ending strife,
A smoke, a blackness from the abyss
Where unclean serpents coil and hiss!
Love is the Holy Ghost within;
Hate the unpardonable sin!
Who preaches otherwise than this,
Betrays his Master with a kiss!

II.

MARTIN LUTHER.

A Chamber in the Wartburg. Morning. MARTIN LUTHER, *writing.*

MARTIN LUTHER.

Our God, a Tower of Strength is he,
A goodly wall and weapon;
From all our need he helps us free,
That now to us doth happen.
    The old evil foe
    Doth in earnest grow,
    In grim armor dight,
    Much guile and great might;
On earth there is none like him.

O yes; a tower of strength indeed,
A present help in all our need,
A sword and buckler is our God.

MARTIN LUTHER.

Innocent men have walked unshod
O'er burning ploughshares, and have trod
Unharmed on serpents in their path,
And laughed to scorn the Devil's wrath!

Safe in this Wartburg tower I stand
Where God hath led me by the hand,
And look down, with a heart at ease,
Over the pleasant neighborhoods,
Over the vast Thuringian Woods,
With flash of river, and gloom of trees,
With castles crowning the dizzy heights,
And farms and pastoral delights,
And the morning pouring everywhere
Its golden glory on the air.
Safe, yes, safe am I here at last,
Safe from the overwhelming blast
Of the mouths of Hell, that followed me fast,
And the howling demons of despair
That hunted me like a beast to his lair.

Of our own might we nothing can;
We soon are unprotected;
There fighteth for us the right Man,
Whom God himself elected.
    Who is he; ye exclaim?
    Christus is his name,
    Lord of Sabaoth,
    Very God in troth;
The field he holds forever.

Nothing can vex the Devil more
Than the name of Him whom we adore.
Therefore doth it delight me best
To stand in the choir among the rest,
With the great organ trumpeting
Through its metallic tubes, and sing:
Et verbum caro factum est!
These words the Devil cannot endure,
For he knoweth their meaning well!
Him they trouble and repel,
Us they comfort and allure,

And happy it were, if our delight
Were as great as his affright!
Yea, music is the Prophets' art;
Among the gifts that God hath sent,
One of the most magnificent!
It calms the agitated heart;
Temptations, evil thoughts, and all
The passions that disturb the soul,
Are quelled by its divine control,
As the Evil Spirit fled from Saul,
And his distemper was allayed,
When David took his harp and played.

  This world may full of Devils be,
  All ready to devour us;
  Yet not so sore afraid are we,
  They shall not overpower us.
    This World's Prince, howe'er
    Fierce he may appear,
    He can harm us not,
    He is doomed, Got wot!
  One little word can slay him!

Incredible it seems to some
And to myself a mystery,
That such weak flesh and blood as we,
Armed with no other shield or sword,
Or other weapon than the Word,
Should combat and should overcome,
A spirit powerful as he!
He summons forth the Pope of Rome
With all his diabolic crew,
His shorn and shaven retinue
Of priests and children of the dark;
Kill! kill! they cry, the Heresiarch,
Who rouseth up all Christendom
Against us; and at one fell blow
Seeks the whole Church to overthrow!
Not yet; my hour is not yet come.

Yesterday in an idle mood,
Hunting with others in the wood,
I did not pass the hours in vain,

For in the very heart of all
The joyous tumult raised around,
Shouting of men, and baying of hound,
And the bugle's blithe and cheery call,
And echoes answering back again,
From crags of the distant mountain chain,—
In the very heart of this, I found
A mystery of grief and pain.
It was an image of the power
Of Satan, hunting the world about,
With his nets and traps and well-trained dogs,
His bishops and priests and theologues,
And all the rest of the rabble rout,
Seeking whom he may devour!
Enough have I had of hunting hares,
Enough of these hours of idle mirth,
Enough of nets and traps and gins!
The only hunting of any worth
Is where I can pierce with javelins
The cunning foxes and wolves and bears
The whole iniquitous troop of beasts,

The Roman Pope and the Roman priests
That sorely infest and afflict the earth!

Ye nuns, ye singing birds of the air!
The fowler hath caught you in his snare,
And keeps you safe in his gilded cage
Singing the song that never tires,
To lure down others from their nests;
How ye flutter and beat your breasts,
Warm and soft with young desires
Against the cruel pitiless wires,
Reclaiming your lost heritage!
Behold! a hand unbars the door,
Ye shall be captives held no more.

    The Word they shall perforce let stand,
    And little thanks they merit!
    For He is with us in the land,
    With gifts of his own Spirit!
        Though they take our life,
        Goods, honors, child and wife,

Let these pass away,
Little gain have they;
The Kingdom still remaineth!

Yea, it remaineth forevermore,
However Satan may rage and roar,
Though often he whispers in my ears:
What if thy doctrines false should be?
And wrings from me a bitter sweat.
Then I put him to flight with jeers,
Saying: Saint Satan! pray for me;
If thou thinkest I'm not saved yet!

And my mortal foes that lie in wait
In every avenue and gate!
As to that odious monk John Tetzel
Hawking about his hollow wares
Like a huckster at village fairs,
And those mischievous fellows, Wetzel,
Campanus, Carlstadt, Martin Cellarius,
And all the busy, multifarious

Heretics, and disciples of Arius,
Half-learned, dunce-bold, dry and hard,
They are not worthy of my regard,
Poor and humble as I am.

But ah! Erasmus of Rotterdam,
He is the vilest miscreant
That ever walked this world below!
A Momus, making his mock and mow,
At papist and at protestant,
Sneering at St. John and St. Paul,
At God and Man, at one and all;
And yet as hollow and false and drear,
As a cracked pitcher to the ear,
And ever growing worse and worse!
Whenever I pray, I pray for a curse
On Erasmus, the Insincere!

Philip Melancthon! thou alone
Faithful among the faithless known,

Thee I hail, and only thee!
Behold the record of us three!
  Res et verba Philippus,
  Res sine verbis Lutherus;
  Erasmus verba sine re!

My Philip, prayest thou for me?
Lifted above all earthly care,
From these high regions of the air,
Among the birds that day and night
Upon the branches of tall trees
Sing their lauds and litanies,
Praising God with all their might,
My Philip, unto thee I write.

My Philip! thou who knowest best
All that is passing in this breast;
The spiritual agonies,
The inward deaths, the inward hell,
And the divine new births as well,

That surely follow after these,
As after winter follows spring;
My Philip, in the night-time sing
This song of the Lord I send to thee;
And I will sing it for thy sake,
Until our answering voices make
A glorious antiphony,
And choral chant of victory!

III.

FINALE.

SAINT JOHN *wandering over the face of the Earth.*

ST. JOHN.

THE Ages come and go,
The Centuries pass as Years;
My hair is white as the snow,
My feet are weary and slow,
The earth is wet with my tears!
The kingdoms crumble, and fall
Apart, like a ruined wall,
Or a bank that is undermined
By a river's ceaseless flow,
And leave no trace behind!
The world itself is old;
The portals of Time unfold

On hinges of iron, that grate
And groan with the rust and the weight,
Like the hinges of a gate
That hath fallen to decay;
But the evil doth not cease;
There is war instead of peace,
Instead of love there is hate;
And still I must wander and wait,
Still I must watch and pray,
Not forgetting in whose sight,
A thousand years in their flight
Are as a single day.

The life of man is a gleam
Of light, that comes and goes
Like the course of the Holy Stream,
The cityless river, that flows
From fountains no one knows,
Through the Lake of Galilee,
Through forests and level lands,
Over rocks, and shallows, and sands

Of a wilderness wild and vast,
Till it findeth its rest at last
In the desolate Dead Sea!
But alas! alas for me,
Not yet this rest shall be!

What, then! doth Charity fail?
Is Faith of no avail?
Is Hope blown out like a light
By a gust of wind in the night?
The clashing of creeds, and the strife
Of the many beliefs, that in vain
Perplex man's heart and brain,
Are naught but the rustle of leaves,
When the breath of God upheaves
The boughs of the Tree of Life,
And they subside again!
And I remember still
The words, and from whom they came,
Not he that repeateth the name,
But he that doeth the will!

And Him evermore I behold
Walking in Galilee,
Through the cornfield's waving gold,
In hamlet, in wood, and in wold,
By the shores of the Beautiful Sea.
He toucheth the sightless eyes;
Before him the demons flee;
To the dead he sayeth: Arise!
To the living: Follow me!
And that voice still soundeth on
From the centuries that are gone,
To the centuries that shall be!

From all vain pomps and shows,
From the pride that overflows,
And the false conceits of men;
From all the narrow rules
And subtleties of Schools,
And the craft of tongue and pen;
Bewildered in its search,
Bewildered with the cry:

ST. JOHN.

Lo, here! lo, there, the Church!
Poor, sad Humanity
Through all the dust and heat
Turns back with bleeding feet,
By the weary road it came,
Unto the simple thought
By the Great Master taught,
And that remaineth still:
Not he that repeateth the name,
But he that doeth the will!

THE END.

www.ingramcontent.com/pod-product-compliance
Lightning Source LLC
Chambersburg PA
CBHW031353230426
43670CB00006B/525